P9-DDI-861

AK47

The Story of a Gun

BY MICHAEL HODGES

NORTH COUNTRY LIBRARY SYSTEM
Watertown, New York

AK47

The Story of a Gun

BY MICHAEL HODGES

CENTRAL LIBRARY
WATERTOWN

MACADAM CAGE

MacAdam/Cage
155 Sansome Street, Suite 550
San Francisco, CA 94104
www.MacAdamCage.com

Copyright © 2007 by Michael Hodges
ALL RIGHTS RESERVED

Library of Congress Cataloging-in-Publication Data

Hodges, Michael.
  AK47 : the story of a gun / by Michael Hodges.
    p. cm.
  ISBN 978-1-59692-286-0
  1. AK-47 rifle. 2. AK-47 rifle—History. I. Title. II. Title: AK-47.
  UD395.A16H63 2008
  623.4'425—dc22

                              2007050970

Cover design by Dorothy Carico Smith
Manufactured in the United States of America

10 9 8 7 6 5 4 3 2 1

First published as *AK47: The Story of the People's Gun* in Great Britain in 2007 by
Hodder & Stoughton, a division of Hodder Headline

With due respect to Emmanuel and Mikhail

TABLE OF CONTENTS

He was wearing khaki dungarees about three sizes too big for him and a boy's shirt with pictures of Mickey Mouse printed across the front. In his right hand he held the barrel of a Kalashnikov.

Robert Fisk, *Pity the Nation*

Let the President answer on high anarchy,
Strap him with an AK47,
Let him go fight his own war.

Eminem, *Mosh*

TIMELINE

1947— Mikhail Kalashnikov wins competition to design new Soviet assault rifle

1949— Soviet Army adopts the AK47

1956— Widespread distribution of AK47 to Eastern European allies. Suppression of Hungarian Revolution by Soviet Army. AK47 factories established in Communist China

1959— Mikhail Kalashnikov unveils the AKM (modernised)

1965— President Lyndon Johnson commits US troops to Vietnam. Chinese supply AK model 56 to Vietnamese Communist Forces. Mass production in China and Eastern Europe increases flow of AKs to Africa and Middle East

1967— Six-Day War, Israel seizes Arab territory including West Bank, Gaza Strip and Golan Heights

1968— Battle of Karameh between Israel Defence Force and Fatah guerillas

1972— Black September group murder eleven Israeli athletes at Munich Olympic games

1973— US ground troops withdraw from Vietnam

1974—	Introduction of AK74, AKM reconfigured to fire smaller 5.45mm round
1978—	AK74 distributed to Eastern European allies
1979—	Soviet invasion of Afghanistan
1983—	State of emergency in Sudan leads to civil war
1989—	Soviet withdrawal from Afghanistan
1991—	Collapse of Soviet Union
1993—	The Battle of Mogadishu (Black Hawk Down incident), Somalia
1994—	Federal Assault Weapons Ban passed by US Congress
1999—	Russian invasion of Chechnya
2000—	Second Intifada breaks out in occupied Palestian territories
2001—	US invasion of Afghanistan
2003—	US invasion of Iraq
2004—	Beslan siege and battle Launch of Kalashnikov vodka in UK

INTRODUCTION

The AK47 should be on the scrap heap of history. Sixty years old and lacking accuracy, it is an antique in comparison to the plastic and carbon assault rifles used by the US and British armies today. The AK47 was not even the first semi-automatic assault weapon on the battlefield—that, arguably, was the German MP43, used against the Russians during the Second World War. Neither was the AK47 the most sophisticated weapon of its era: the gas-operated bolt-firing system was basic technology even for the 1940s. However, it is the AK47's very simplicity that has powered its success. With only eight moving parts, it is both cheap to manufacture and easy to use; indeed, so easy that any combatant, child or adult, can put down a devastating 650 rounds-per-minute rate of fire after very basic training. The AK47 can be stripped in under a minute and cleaned quickly in almost any climatic conditions. Even if it isn't cleaned, an AK47 is still more likely to fire than any of its rivals given similar treatment on the battlefield.

These attributes have propelled its journey through the three stages this book will follow. First, as the gun that enabled the Soviet Union to control the vast territories it had acquired through victory over Nazi Germany; second, as the icon of Third World revolution; and finally, in the hands of Osama bin Laden, as the brand leader for international terrorism and the most ubiquitous gun in the world.

Turn on the radio or television news and you will hear a reporter talking of assailants carrying Kalashnikov-type assault rifles or insurgents armed with AK47s. Pick up any broadsheet or tabloid newspaper and you will find at least one photograph of an AK47. Often the picture will be on the front page; sometimes it will be hidden inside on the international news pages; but even if you know nothing of guns you will instinctively recognize the distinctive curve of the Kalashnikov's ammunition magazine.

The AK might be in the hands of an Iraqi government soldier or rebel, an Afghan Mujahadeen, a Colombian militiaman, a Palestinian gunman or an African child soldier. The first real AK47 I saw was in the hands of a fighter in the South Lebanon Army, on the border between his country and Israel, in May 1982. The Christian militiaman was sitting on the open back of a pick-up truck that was zigzagging along a dirt track on the Lebanese side of the border, attempting to avoid mortars that were being fired from a Palestinian position. The Israelis I was with laughed at the militiaman's defiance, and I suppose it was funny in a way to see a lone man waving his gun at the people who were trying to kill him. But I didn't laugh—unlike the Israelis I had never before seen real bullets being fired or real bombs being dropped, and I was hypnotized by the man in the speeding truck holding his AK in the air as the explosives burst around him. There was something unique about his gun—not just the way it looked, but something else. At the age of eighteen I realized that the AK47 wasn't like other weapons: it had an atmosphere.

Implausible? Perhaps. The famous set of initials and numbers is prosaic enough, the result of a simple military process that produced scores of other letters and numbers in the mid-twentieth-century Soviet Union: weapons such as the TT-33, PPS 1943 and PPSh 1941. The 4 and the 7 signify the year of the gun's invention. The A stands for the sort of rifle it is, *avtomat* in Russian, and automatic in English. And K is the first letter of the inventor's surname: Kalashnikov.

When I first met General Mikhail Kalashnikov in Russia he called it a 'Golem' after the animated imp of Yiddish legend—it was a gun, he admitted, that had left the orbit of its creators and become a force in itself. So we have reason to be fearful of its powers as there are, according to conservative UN estimates, 70 million Kalashnikovs in worldwide use: a staggering number and almost certainly an underestimate by several millions. Consequently I cannot even attempt to cover in this book every conflict in which the gun is, or has been, used; to do so would take many volumes, and the work would be out-of-date as soon as it was finished. So I have attempted to follow the Golem's journey through those conflicts from which the atmosphere it engenders can best be gauged, in countries where the Kalashnikov is both history and, unfortunately, the future.

Two months after I watched that Lebanese militiaman being driven through mortar bombs with his AK47 held high in the air, the Israel Defence Force invaded and drove his Palestinian tormentors from southern Lebanon. As the IDF advanced they captured thousands of Palestinian AK47s. These guns found their way via the CIA and the Pakistani secret service to the Mujahadeen in Afghanistan, to fight the soldiers of the Kalashnikov's motherland. Amongst the vast arms caches would have been the first AK47 that Osama bin Laden picked up, perhaps even the weapon that featured in the video made by the leader of Al-Queda to claim responsibility for the 9/11 attacks on the United States.

Is there too much irony at work here to be believable? As we shall find out, the AK47 is that kind of gun.

THE KILLING JOKE

'I can get you in the factory. No problem.'

The speaker was a short man in his early fifties, olive-skinned and dressed smartly in a sports jacket and shirt. It was August 2004. I had been in Izhevsk, home city of the Kalashnikov and its inventor, for only a few hours and I was about to get access to the buildings where millions of AKs had been made since the late 1940s. Even though I was drunk, the offer seemed too good to be true.

'Won't it be difficult getting into a government arms plant in the middle of the night?' I enquired.

'No problem! This is the best time to go in—they will be having fun. We can have a banya.'

'Banya?'

'Yes—a steam bath, and more vodka!' His English was excellent, with only the faintest trace of an accent, but all I knew of the man I had met in a bar two hours and many drinks earlier was that he claimed to be in Izhevsk on business and he came from the Caucasus. Just what might be going on in a Kalashnikov factory at one o'clock in the morning I wasn't sure, but we were several bottles of vodka down the line and right now fun seemed like a very good idea.

He called a cab, and we drove through the empty streets and Soviet-era boulevards of the once mighty city before turning down a broad road that ran alongside a large lake, glinting in the moonlight that broke through the clouds. I couldn't see the water that lapped against the embankment, but it had been rusty and brackish for two hundred years, stained red by millions of tons of iron slag. It wasn't a lake but a reservoir, dug on the orders of Tsar Alexander I in 1810 to supply the millions of gallons of water required by the city's giant foundries. Izhevsk men forged the weapons that, along with the Russian winter, turned back Napoleon's Grande Armée in 1812. Their cannon roared across the chaos and confusion of the battle of Borodino and harried the French in their terrible retreat from Moscow. So that the city would never forget it had beaten Napoleon, the captured standards and flagpoles of the French regiments were cast in iron and mounted on the gable ends of the main foundry building.

From this triumphal beginning more foundries and, as technology advanced, steel-pressing plants grew during the nineteenth century, and further expansion took place during the First World War. After 1920 three giant arms plants were developed under the Soviets, and when arms production was moved east in the face of Nazi invasion in 1941 Izhevsk swelled into a city of seven hundred thousand workers. The factories covered more than 13 square kilometres and were so large, and the thousands of workers inside so productive, that Izhevsk produced more small arms during the Second World War than every factory in the German Reich combined. By 1945 the city could count Hitler as well as Napoleon amongst the dictators it had defeated. This achievement alone was enough for it to earn the 'fraternal and eternal' gratitude of its sister cities in the Union of Soviet Socialist Republics, but it was famous within Russia for more than its Stakhanovite war efforts. Izhevsk had another, even more important, claim to eminence. As the cab turned into the vast Izhmash plant I felt a thrill of recognition and excitement, even though my head was beginning to swim; this was the AK47's home ground, the factory where the gun's inventor, Mikhail Kalashnikov, and a brilliant team of Soviet weapons engineers had adapted and fine-tuned the weapon that had come to dominate the world.

But there was no sign of the AK's former glory. True, alongside the road ran at least a kilometre of iron railings behind which stood grandiose early nineteenth-century neo-classical porticos; however, behind that façade things changed dramatically. We drove slowly between looming assembly buildings, past smashed windows and empty doorways, through once pristine yards that were now ramshackle. Sixty years after the AK47's invention Izhevsk was no longer a Soviet city but the capital of the Russian Federation Republic of Udmurtia and, despite the unrelenting worldwide demand for assault rifles, the city that had out-produced Adolf Hitler's Reich was dying on its feet. There were no lights showing in the great industrial complex where millions of AKs had once rolled off the production lines. Around the world the gun was more popular than ever, but there was no dividend for Izhevsk. Even though the Russians had been trying hard to rescue the city's fortunes, other states were cashing in on the demand for its best-known product.

In 2003 the US government, long convinced of the Kalashnikov's efficiency after gruelling encounters with it during the Vietnam War and in the Middle East, had awarded the contract to supply AKs for the reformed Iraqi security forces to the Bulgarian state weapons maker, Arsenal. The Russian state export agency, Rosoboronexport, complained, arguing that 'These products should be bought at the factories where they were first developed.' But the Bulgarians were selling their Kalashnikovs for US $100; the cheapest modern Russian models were US $500. Izhmash, the plant 'where they were first developed', was no longer a major producer—the remaining assembly lines were mostly turning out limited lines of the specialized hunting and sports rifles that the general had designed in the 1980s and 1990s, and were producing no more than three thousand Kalashnikov assault rifles a year. The men and women who had once maintained the Soviet Union's small arms superiority over the United States were now unemployed. They sat on park benches or outside bars where they could watch the small parties of American gun enthusiasts who turned up for guided tours of the Izhevsk factory, wearing 'Kalashnikov World Tour' t-shirts that listed the war-torn countries and regions where the AK had inflicted terror. Local people turned to other ways of earning an income: there were money-changers working out of aging Ladas on petrol station forecourts, and lank-haired young men selling the startlingly strong local dope in bars. The young people looked for an identity in Udmurtian folk music and paganism rather than in Russian nationalism. The re-cast totems of Napoleon's defeat were still mounted on the factory roof, but now they looked down on a city on the edge of decay.

As we drove round it that night the plant seemed deserted, and I noted that there weren't even any security patrols. It was at this moment that my new friend leaned over from the front seat and revealed which part of the Caucasus he was from. 'I'm an Azerbaijani. The guards might be nervous if they see my face.'

'Why?'

'They might think I'm a Chechen. You know, a terrorist. They might shoot me. If we meet any guards it's best to show them your passport first.'

It occurred to me that I had no real idea who this man was and that we were driving through what was supposed to be a sensitive military establishment. This might be less fun than I had hoped. Before I could act on my fears we turned a corner and encountered a closed gate and the first human being we had seen since entering the complex—a soldier wearing a khaki blouson over a hooped blue and white t-shirt. An AK was slung over his shoulder and he was smoking a spliff. He gestured for the car to slow down.

'Passport! Passport!' urged my Azeri friend. I leaned forward and held it up through the front passenger window. The soldier looked at it without blinking before opening the gate and waving our car through.

'See, it's fine,' said my companion, and we continued past more derelict buildings and under a fly-over. The driver, who had clearly made this night-time journey many times before, negotiated a succession of sharp corners and turns before coming to a halt before a wooden chalet that looked more Swiss than Russian and was bathed in soft yellow light.

'Here we are,' said the Azeri, who appeared to be very relieved for a man who had claimed that getting here would be easy. He bounded up to the door, where a Russian woman in her mid-fifties with dyed black hair was standing. They turned inside and I followed them into a small reception room. Suddenly I realized that all that vodka had made me feel more ill than I would have expected, and I went over to an open window to get some air.

Laughter from the Azeri and the Russian woman broke my reverie; she took me by the arm and pushed me through a second, inner door into what I assumed must be the banya itself. I expected to find something military—interior decoration that made reference to what went on, or had gone on, here. Perhaps a bar decorated with pictures of Russian soldiers, or an original AK47 mounted on a wall and a room full of drunken men in towels talking about rate of fire and accuracy. But it was a very different scene that confronted me. In the centre was a large round table with eight seats around it. Armchairs and sofas were scattered about the edge of the room, and in one corner stood a large flat-screen television showing American pop videos. A tall fridge with a glass door was stocked with champagne, beer, vodka and caviar. In another corner a staircase led up to an open upper floor where I could see more doors leading off to other rooms. An exit beside the fridge, I presumed, was the door to the banya. There were certainly no pictures of soldiers or AKs. All the walls were lined with wood and, rather than men in towels, girls wearing miniskirts and plunging tops slouched moodily on the chairs.

'Come,' invited the Azeri, 'enjoy yourself.'

A bottle of vodka was opened and I took a seat. Immediately an attractive blonde with a round face and a little English ('Hello…I like you') sat by my side, poured me a drink and started to talk in Russian.

Pretty though she was, I wasn't looking at her but at the vodka bottle she had put down on the table. Written across the top of the label in Cyrillic script was one word: 'Kalashnikov'. Beneath it was a picture of a young Soviet serviceman in Second World War uniform.

The girl turned my face to hers and asked, 'Do you want to go upstairs?'

I shook my head and said, with ridiculous primness, 'No, I'm here to work, and I just want a drink, thank you.'

'What business are you here for?'

I pointed at the bottle. 'For the gun.'

'What gun?'

'The Kalashnikov. I'm here to find out about the AK47.'

The girl looked a little disappointed; although she was working in what had once been the heart of the Kalashnikov's world, she wasn't interested in guns. The AK was history and, like all the other young people in Izhevsk, she was only interested in the future. She stood up and pulled at my hand. 'Come now, we go upstairs.'

'No, really, thank you, but I'm fine.'

Unimpressed, she went and sat with the other girls nearer the television. Presumably she told them that I didn't like blondes, because a girl with dark shoulder-length hair and shiny knee-high black boots then came over. She lifted the bottle and glugged more syrupy, chilled vodka into my glass. I watched the Azeri go upstairs with two of her colleagues. The girl with the dark hair gestured for me to follow, but I smiled and said no again. She looked at me as though I was a specimen in a glass jar and as the spirit reached my stomach I started to feel like one. The remaining girls turned their attention away from me and towards an aging soft rock outfit on the television, and as the middle-aged men on the screen huffed and puffed through their song the Kalashnikov vodka bottle floated before my eyes and gradually I felt Izhevsk and the girls slip away.

The next morning came unpleasantly and late. I had no memory of how I had got back to the guesthouse, but I had missed breakfast. Skull aching and stomach rumbling, I got into a taxi and headed for a very important lunch appointment.

General Mikhail Timofeyevich Kalashnikov's dacha lay six kilometres away from Izhevsk on the other side of the reservoir. I was met at the garden gate by the general's grandson Igor, who, as he led me to the two-storey wooden house, proudly pointed out gadgets and improvements that his grandfather had made with his own hand.

'You see that sprinkler there? He installed it. And outside here, on the porch, this is the bread bin he made.'

Inside, a corridor led to an open central room where a table was laid out for lunch. The eighty-five-year-old was waiting at the foot of the stairs. He was wearing sharply creased grey slacks, a white shirt buttoned up to the collar, a brown cardigan and a pair of fun fur leopardskin ankle slippers. Almost as soon as he had welcomed me he appeared to dampen my expectations.

'This book will be very difficult, maybe impossible. You see, guns aren't about designers—we just invent them. It's politicians who decide who gets the guns, and the politicians won't talk about it.' But I would soon find that the only person who had problems talking about the AK47 was the general himself.

He gestured for me to go into the kitchen where his housekeeper was making elk soup. Just as stripping an AK47 has a correct order—release magazine catch, remove magazine, cock rifle, release catch on the right side of rear sight, push piston assembly cover forward and detach from piston assembly and bolt—there was a fixed way of making the general's soup. First his housekeeper softened some onions by frying them in a little vegetable oil, and then she added stock from the ribs of an elk the general had shot himself. The broth was simmered for an hour, and at the end cabbage leaves were added. When the soup was poured into a tureen diced spring onions and soured cream were floated on the surface. The housekeeper talked as she cooked.

'He is very particular about the stock. He boils it himself from the elk's ribs and says to me, "Taste this! I guarantee that this is the best stock that you have ever tasted—even better than the last stock I made."'

The general laughed and commented, 'But things have to be right!'

'Yes,' I agreed. 'That's why I am very keen to hear your version of the gun's story.'

He mulled this over for a moment, then said, laughing, 'But we must eat!' And with that he motioned me towards the table where we drank the first of what would be many toasts that afternoon. 'To friendship!' he shouted, knocking his glass against mine. And somehow I kept it down.

Kalashnikov had good reason to look pleased with himself. Stalin, Khrushchev, Brezhnev, Yeltsin and Putin had all honoured him. Twice, in 1958 and 1976, he had been acclaimed a Hero of Socialist Labour. He had been awarded the Stalin Prize First Class in 1949, had been a recipient of the Lenin Prize in 1964 and claimed a further three Orders of Lenin, the Order of the Red Banner of Labour, the Order of the Great Patriotic War (First Class) and an Order of the Red Star. Along with the medals there had there been a propaganda campaign that celebrated this proletarian genius whose achievements proved the superiority of Soviet communism. In 1948 articles appeared in *Pravda* and Soviet armed forces newspapers, praising the heroic young tank commander who had invented a gun to beat fascism—despite the fact that the AK would not go into service until four years after the destruction of Hitler's Germany. More than half a century later this was still the general's justification. 'I invented a weapon to save my motherland,' he said, wiping up the last of the elk soup with some bread, 'to save the state from fascism. My career has been dedicated to my country.'

Spending time with the general, I would come to realize that for him the AK47 was not only the weapon that he had invented to save Russia but the ultimate symbol of the Russia he had aimed to save. In some ways, time had stopped for him in the late 1940s. He had gone on to engineer further developments in Soviet small arms—in fact some of his finest work lay ahead of him—but the warm glow of victory in the Second World War and the first successes of the AK47 had cemented the period as a golden time in his memory. Thousands of Soviet citizens had suffered terribly during the war and afterwards as Stalin descended into his final, violently paranoid years, but for the general 'It was a time when all the races of the Soviet Union came together to stop Hitler. We lived together in brotherhood then, everyone fought for each other. Everyone made great sacrifices, but we were happy to do it. In those days we were a united country. It did not matter what race you were, a Tartar or a Ukrainian, you were dedicated to the motherland.'

The AK47 had brought him many medals, but it had earned him little money. Unlike the multi-millionaire inventor of the American M16, Eugene Stoner—a man who was little known outside the world of arms design but who had made millions from his invention—Kalashnikov had no copyright or financial deal on his invention. Stoner earned commission on each rifle, whereas Kalashnikov was surviving on a monthly state pension that was the equivalent of US $300. In his long and eventful life he had known far worse hardships than being short of cash, but now he needed money to leave to his grandchildren, who would not be able to live off his Orders of Lenin and the Great Patriotic War when he died.

In Russia Kalashnikov earned a few dollars by lending his name to the bottle I had looked at queasily the night before—naming vodka after famous men is a long-established tradition in Russia, where it is also possible to buy bottles of Vladimir Putin or Boris Yeltsin. And now he had given his support to British businessman John Florey who, convinced that the Kalashnikov name would be marketing dynamite in the West and elsewhere, had brought together a group of British investors to buy the rights to distribute the vodka outside Russia. In September 2004 the general was due in London, to celebrate the European launch of Kalashnikov vodka. Aware that, as well as a sense of authentic Russianness, the name Kalashnikov brought with it other, less attractive, associations such as terror and death, Florey and his group were focussing their pitch on the tradition inherent within Kalashnikov's personal history: comradeship, trustworthiness, quality. To emphasize the universal nature of these attributes, the launch would be dressed in the clothes of English tradition. On his arrival the general would be the guest of honour at a ceremonial dinner given by the Household Cavalry and there would be a reception at Purdey of St James's, the two-hundred-year-old purveyor of firearms to the British royal family.

The general's visit to London was still four weeks away and, sitting over the remains of the soup, I wondered how he felt about having his image used in this way. At least, I suggested, it was an improvement on the barrage of criticism he usually received. In western Europe and the USA the Soviet Union didn't signify, as it did for the general, order and fraternity, but mass murder and totalitarianism. Kalashnikov's image was fixed as that of death's great designer and few outside the former Soviet bloc listened when he said he abhorred the idea of his weapon being used against civilians or when he called, as he has on several occasions, for the collection and destruction of all the AKs in the world. This was a position he still maintained fiercely across the lunch table.

'How could I realize how long the AK would last or what it would do in the world? But now, I realize well enough. The AK was once my baby, but it has gone out of my control. I can't bring that baby up—it has grown up already. I do not like to see children firing my weapons in Africa or anywhere else, but who put the weapons in their hands? Of course there are casualties. Any war involves killing people, but killing civilians is an illegal use of a weapon. It doesn't matter who makes the arms. Guns should only be brought out in cases of emergency or national threat.'

Emergency and national threat are subjective criteria, and as the general spoke men were finding good reason to bring out their AKs around the world. In Iraq gunmen of the Mehdi Army were firing AKs at US troops from the rooftops of Sadr City. Throughout sub-Saharan Africa scores of conflicts were waxing and waning, their intensity depending often on the availability of Kalashnikovs. In the occupied West Bank Palestinian guerrillas were firing at Israeli Merkava tanks, and in Kashmir separatist guerrillas were ambushing the Indian army with AKs. In Pakistan Pathan tribesmen were firing AKs at Pakistani border guards, and in the Himalayas Maoist insurgents were firing AKs at Nepalese police. And in a cave somewhere in the Hindu Kush Osama bin Laden was sitting in front of a video camera with an AK by his side.

It was hard to make a direct connection between all that carnage and the small, dapper man sitting in his dacha by the reservoir. But many have tried, and the general is wary of Western, especially British, journalists since a BBC documentary in the late 1990s portrayed him, as he put it, 'as a monster, an inveterate war criminal' rather than as an engineer who had resolved complicated technical problems with brilliant simplicity.

Yet if the general and the proprietors of Kalashnikov vodka thought that any perceived link with bin Laden in the public imagination was their most pressing PR concern they were wrong. There was indeed a threat to the coming launch, but it was much closer to home than events in the Middle East or New York. It came from a band of utterly ruthless killers in a small Caucasian republic who were determined to leave the Russian Federation: Chechnya.

When communism fell in 1991 the Russian state contracted temporarily. In the face of this chaos and uncertainty many of the ex-Soviet republics on the periphery took the opportunity to break away. Those republics that were culturally least Russian or Orthodox Christian broke hardest. As Russia lost control it left behind the vast armoury of the Soviet Union that would fuel bitter local conflicts created by the fears of the ruling elites and the desires of the indigenous populations. These conflicts, supercharged by the presence of so many rifles, spiralled into savage wars, wars characterized by the indiscriminate slaughter of civilians with Kalashnikovs.

In the face of such instability in the important oil-producing region of the Caucasus Russia's disengagement process quickly came to a halt, and its policy increasingly came to resemble that of a colonial power playing off small states and ethnic groups against each other. This, as it had been in the time of the tsars, was invariably a matter of supporting Christians against Muslims. In 1992 the Russian army's 366th Motor Rifle Regiment, armed with AK47s, fought alongside the Christian Armenian army as it massacred hundreds of Muslim Azerbaijani civilians in the disputed region of Nagorno-Karabakh. The newly liberalized Russian media was able to show pictures of the slaughter to a horrified Russian public. Watching in Izhevsk, Mikhail Kalashnikov saw the peoples of his motherland turning on each other with the machine he had invented to defend them. It moved him to proffer his first public words of unease with the ubiquity and use of the AK47: 'Do you think it's pleasant seeing all those hoodlums using your gun? Armenians and Azeris killing each other. We all lived so peacefully before.'

But the Armenians and the Azeris, like the ethnic populations in the rest of the Caucasus, had a centuries-old tradition of killing one another. There had merely been a seventy-five-year hiatus imposed by the Soviet state—a state that killed on an altogether larger and more industrial scale. The Caucasus would be an exemplar of how an initially small-scale dispute twinned with a large-scale supply of Kalashnikovs can turn swiftly to carnage. As the conflict was in an ex-Soviet republic, it was inevitable that any military intervention by Russian forces would see those forces go into combat against the AK47. Thousands of Russian servicemen had been killed by AK fire in the ten-year-long conflict in Afghanistan from 1979, but the wars of the 1990s would be a new experience for a demoralized conscript army that was facing fighters who were often more adept at using the Russian national weapon than the Russians were themselves. Soviet dissemination of the AK throughout the school system and then military conscription had been so complete that it was just as much Kazakh or Uzbek as it was Russian. Chechen separatists would exploit this equal ownership of the Kalashnikov to the point where they became the leading threat to the security, and arguably the existence, of Russian democracy.

The Chechens had been fighting domination by Moscow since 1604, when a Russian army under Tsar Boris Godunov was seen off after a year-long attempt to subjugate the region. In 1944 Stalin accused the Chechens and their neighbouring Ingush kinsmen of collaborating with the German invaders who threatened the Caucasus and its oilfields. Stalin's punishment was mass deportation: four hundred thousand Chechen and Ingush were transferred to Kazakhstan and Siberia (the initial part of the journey in trucks supplied by the USA to help the war effort against Nazi Germany). As it happened, the trains rumbled directly past the Kazakhstan workshops where the twenty-two-year-old Kalashnikov was working on his first, unsuccessful, attempt to create an automatic weapon for the Red Army. The period of exile lasted until 1957, when Khrushchev allowed the Chechens to come home. But the returnees found that their homes had been seized by Russian immigrants and the streets of the capital, Grozny, were patrolled by Soviet policemen and soldiers carrying AK47s. Sullenly but watchfully, the Chechens settled back to life as a subject people of the Soviet Union and waited for their moment.

And as they waited their children, like the children in all the other Soviet republics, were taught to strip an AK in under a minute at high school. The Chechens' time came with the collapse of the Soviet Union in 1991. An ex-Soviet air force general, Jokhar Dudayev, was amongst the first leaders in the Caucasus to realize that national self-determination was now possible but would have to be won violently. He immediately used Chechen units of the Soviet army to grab thousands of Kalashnikovs in storage in Grozny and took over key government institutions there, including the KGB headquarters, in what was effectively a Kalashnikov putsch.

After a period of negotiation and increasing levels of banditry outside Grozny, in 1994 President Boris Yeltsin sent in the Russian army to 'restore order'. The twenty months of full-scale war that followed resulted in over a hundred thousand deaths and forced the Chechens and their AKs on to Russian soil. When in 1995 Chechen rebels seized a hospital in Budennovsk in Russia, ninety-four civilians were killed in the raid and the ensuing attempt by Russian commandos to regain the hospital. Again, the majority of the victims died from Kalashnikov fire.

In 1999 Chechen fighters killed three hundred Russians in separate bomb and Kalashnikov attacks, Russian troops clashed with Chechen fighters in Dagestan, south of Chechnya, and eventually the Russian army flattened the reoccupied Grozny. But as before, when the Russians attempted to bomb the Chechens into submission they took cover until the bombardment finished and then walked out of the ruins holding their AK47s. When the Russian army and Chechen guerrillas did meet directly, it was usually at a time and a place of the guerrillas' choosing. The Chechens were increasingly joined by Islamic fighters who were veterans of the Soviet-Afghan War and able to apply the lessons learned in that conflict. Mountain passes and valleys became the scenes of regular ambushes, with a severe cost to Russia's predominantly conscript army. By the late 1990s there were no safe areas for the Russian army in Chechnya.

Behind every bush, tree or rock there was a Chechen with a Kalashnikov.

In 1997, the fiftieth anniversary of the AK47's invention, President Yeltsin visited Izhevsk and presented Kalashnikov with a ceremonial pistol. The general said with some justification, 'As soon as someone invents a better assault rifle, I will shake his hand. But it has not happened yet.' In a quieter moment he wondered, 'Can it be that I have sacrificed so much, only for Chechens to put my assault rifle into new-born babies' cradles the way they formerly put a sabre or a dagger there?' The short and brutal answer to which was: yes.

The Chechens were fighting a guerrilla war, a form of combat to which the Kalashnikov, impervious to dirt and offering awesome firepower, was uniquely suited. The Russians too were fighting with Kalashnikovs, and although the Chechens used versions that were often ten or more years older the killing joke for the Russian army was that out-of-date AKs were so good it didn't matter. Denied an urban platform in Chechnya, the guerrillas increasingly brought their battle and their AK47s deep into the Russian Federation. Because of the Chechens' utter determination, disregard for any casualties they caused and apparent disinterest in being regarded as freedom fighters rather than terrorists, the gun they carried would take on the mantle of the fighters themselves. In the hands of Chechen separatists the AK became evil. In July 2002, visiting an AK47 exhibition in Suhl in eastern Germany, Kalashnikov told German journalists, 'I'm proud of my invention, but I'm sad that terrorists use it. I would have preferred to invent a machine that people could use and that would help farmers with their work. For example, a lawnmower.'

A week before the general's scheduled arrival in London it was still not certain that he would be able to make the visit. His heartbeat had been erratic, so his Russian doctors insisted he rest for a few days. Kalashnikov therefore took it easy at the dacha. He chatted to his grandson Igor, ate cabbage soup, sipped Chilean Merlot rather than vodka and watched some television. Meanwhile in London Household Cavalry troopers were polishing the regimental silver and Purdey's staff were preparing their Mayfair showrooms for the occasion.

Elsewhere, other preparations were under way, as thirty-two Chechen separatists carrying homemade bombs and AK47s stole into the town of Beslan in neighbouring Ossetia. When the general switched on his television on 1 September 2004 he saw dismaying news: Middle School No. 1 in Beslan had been taken over by Chechen guerrillas. They had seized 1156 hostages, the majority of whom were schoolchildren, and they were demanding an end to the Russian occupation of their homeland. All Russian television broadcasts from Beslan were effectively under the control of the Kremlin; however, the Kremlin was not effectively in control of the siege at Beslan.

Once again the horrified world saw the distinctive curved-magazine profile of the AK47 on its screens, and once more the accompanying message was terror. In the packed sports hall where the hostages were being held, patrolling terrorists carried Kalashnikovs. Outside, besieging groups of Russian Special Forces and regional security officers were holding AKs. And, disastrously, the impromptu militia formed by townspeople were also armed with Kalashnikovs.

The reporters repeated the platitudes and half-truths that had been emanating from the panicked Russian leadership: 'The situation is under control', 'There are only 350 hostages', and 'There are no plans to storm the building.' But outside Middle School No. 1 there were chaotic scenes as disparate groups of regional security forces and paramilitary police milled about by a cordon put up around the school grounds. Amongst these older, beer-bellied men could be spotted slim, balaclava-wearing Russian Special Forces sent in by the Ministry of the Interior along with elite Russian army Spetsnaz units. As a metaphor for the collapse of Russian centralized authority the chaotic situation could hardly have been bettered: the chain of command was breaking down, and you did not have to be a general to see that mayhem was imminent.

What General Kalashnikov could not see was the scene inside Middle School No. 1, where hundreds of terrified children were crushed at AK point into the school gymnasium along with mothers and grandmothers who sat transfixed with fear and exhaustion. Any doubt about the guerrillas' intent was dispelled when they denied their captives drinking water. As the temperature increased in the gymnasium children stripped to their underwear and drank urine to avoid dehydration. According to some local accounts, it was the rage of the local militia that sparked the AK fire-fight that led the terrorists to detonate their mines and bring about a madly cack-handed denouement with 334 deaths, including 186 children. Whatever the cause, the fighting left many small corpses showing the massive physical trauma caused when an AK47 is fired at close range into a running child.

Meanwhile, Mikhail Kalashnikov's heart started to beat regularly again, and on 20 September 2004 he arrived in London. Acting in his new role as honorary chairman of the Kalashnikov Joint Stock Vodka Company, he stood up and addressed the company's board and shareholders who had gathered at a private members' club on Shaftesbury Avenue to celebrate the launch in the United Kingdom of Kalashnikov military strength vodka. Kalashnikov, who was wearing the full-dress uniform of a Russian general, declared: 'I am particularly pleased to be here with people I regard as serious businessmen. I hope this brand is as successful around the world as my gun has been.' The implicit suggestion was that the AK47 was itself just a brand and as such operated like any other brand: free of moral or ethical restraints, a signifier merely of lifestyle choices.

A director of the company rose to thank Kalashnikov and drew attention to the Orders of Lenin that the general held—which led to rapturous applause from the gathering of businessmen, nearly all of whom were products of the English public school system. Beslan went unmentioned at the dinner with the Household Cavalry and at the Purdey's reception. In fact the week passed without any newspaper asking the general about the use of his weapon, so apparent in the television pictures beamed from the siege. However, they all gave valuable space to Kalashnikov vodka. John Florey claimed that 'it has been a very successful visit so far. We were worried that some of the press would be negative but most of the publicity has been fantastic.'

And mainly it was; at worst there was only muted criticism of the link between alcohol and an assault rifle. Even American anti-gun activist group the Brady Campaign to Prevent Gun Violence was gentle. 'We'd hope the general would agree that his weapon was never intended for civilian use, just as he would agree that his vodka should be consumed responsibly. Obviously we hope he'd agree that the people enjoying his vodka should not have anything to do with his weapons.'

Perhaps not so obviously. At the Purdey's reception much of the general's vodka was enjoyed and his weapon was handed around between giggling PR girls and half-cut journalists with relish. The general appeared once again in Soviet-era dress uniform, complete with the Order of Lenin on his chest. A member of the Purdey family, previously unknown for their commitment to Marxist-Leninism, raised a glass of vodka and toasted the 'Kalashnikov and Purdey families' shared traditions'. The general continued to smile; if he was uncomfortable with the signifiers of Soviet brotherhood being reduced to a marketing ploy—a brand marker for the quality of vodka—he was careful not to show it. 'After all,' as one of the directors of the new company said to me, 'who wouldn't want to drink the same vodka as a Hero of Socialist Labour?' In the bonhomie and buzz of the reception it was easy to forget about Beslan; no one was thinking about the AK47 as an actual machine that killed children. Instead, the excited investors and PR girls were thinking of the brand's really revolutionary properties, the fact that they had the 'white spirits equivalent of Che Guevara' on their hands.

But a month later the bottom fell out of the general's attempt to top up his pension. The Portman Group, a self-policing unit set up by the British drinks industry to protect itself from unfavourable government legislation, received the following complaint from Scottish charity Alcohol Focus Scotland: 'The brand name "Kalashnikov" is entirely inappropriate for an alcoholic drink, as the general public would immediately associate the name with the world-famous weapon, the AK-47, which has become a global symbol for terror and violence.' Florey stoutly refuted the charge that Kalashnikov vodka glamorized guns; but the complaint was upheld,

effectively making the product unmarketable in the United Kingdom.

One can only wonder at a sixty-year-old rifle maintaining such a visceral ability to unsettle. The general, as he rightly says, only invented a gun—so who, or rather what, is actually responsible for the AK47's present status as a pre-eminent symbol of terror and liberation as well as being the most ubiquitous small arm in the world? Is it the gun's undoubted prowess as a killing machine? Its brilliantly simple technology and ease of manufacture? The unrelenting supply of Kalashnikovs by communist and post-communist states (and, eventually, the USA) to the Third World for over four decades? Or the power of the gun's revolutionary image—created as much by Western intellectuals as by Third World revolutionaries—and the constant dissemination of that image via mass media?

All have their part to play but in the end the AK's unique success, if success it is, lies in a combination of these factors. By the late 1960s it had developed, alongside its physical attributes, a cultural velocity that was to prove both irresistible and catastrophic for thousands of people, civilians and soldiers, children and adults, men and women. But to get to that point the AK47 had to travel a long journey, a journey that started many years before in the shadow of a war many times more terrible than the conflict in Chechnya.

Soviet communism finally triumphed over German fascism on 30 April 1945, when two Red Army sergeants raised a hammer and sickle banner above the burning Reichstag building in the heart of Berlin. It was the supreme moment of Soviet triumph and even now, long after the collapse of communism, it remains the defining moment of Russian arms.

The sergeants, recruited for the picture by photographer Yevgeni Khaldei and drunk on vodka when they climbed on to the roof, were not carrying AK47s. They had fought their way to the centre of the Reich with PPSh4s, the 'Tommy gun'-style machine gun that had become the signature weapon of the Soviet infantryman. It was the Germans they had just vanquished who carried an assault rifle with a curved ammunition magazine.

It is self-evident to Russians that the AK47's creation was a product of the struggle against fascism, and any claim that the Soviet Union copied German Nazi weaponry still causes anger and discomfort. National pride and collective bitterness at the sheer scale of the losses endured and the sacrifice made by the Soviet people during the Second World War have barely lessened over sixty years, and to question the mythology that has grown around the war is still to put yourself at odds with Russian national feeling. But questions remain over the degree to which German arms technology influenced what has come to stand as the epitome of Russian technological inventiveness. What if the Soviet Union's greatest achievement in small arms was in part a creation of its vanquished and bestial enemy? And what if the man who invented the rifle was no Soviet hero at all, but a criminal fugitive from the communist state?

In September 1946 officials of the special commission of the Soviet People's Commissariat on Armaments welcomed the weapons designer V. A. Degtyarev to the Kovrov weapons plant, 250 kilometres south-east of Moscow. Degtyarev was a legendary arms designer: Soviet infantrymen carried rifles he had designed, and his heavy machine guns armed the country's tanks, fighters and bombers. Now in his late sixties, he had thinning hair and the grey skin of a man who had been overworked for months. He wore the uniform of a full general in the Red Army, with the gold star of a Hero of the Soviet Union pinned to his chest. His gloved hand grasped the handle of a brown leather case which contained the prototype of a semi-automatic gun, his entry into the competition run by the People's Commissariat to equip the army with an assault rifle. It was a competition he was widely expected to win.

The reception committee greeted Degtyarev with the deference he deserved, but as he stepped out of his staff car it was not with the bearing of a man at the height of his achievements. Nodding absent-mindedly as he was shown around the testing facilities and shooting ranges, he only half-listened as the officials updated him on the latest ballistic testing and fire rate reports and he barely looked up as they walked through the workshops where technicians were shaping the future of Soviet small arms. They looked at each other behind the general's back. Why was he so distracted? What was on the old man's mind?

The officials would have been surprised to learn that Degtyarev's mind was on a problem that so far seemed insurmountable—his rifle didn't work. In testing it had either misfired or not fired at all, and even though Degtyarev had tried several different reconfigurations of the rifle's firing mechanism barrel he could not cure the fault. For weeks he had searched his mind for a way to stop the new 7.62 x 39mm cartridge that all the competitors were using from jamming in the firing chamber, and for the first time in his career he could not find a solution.

As the party reached the end of the tour, Degtyarev paused in front of a workbench where a man in his late twenties was standing with two colleagues. The general recognized Mikhail Kalashnikov, an ex-tank commander who had designed a machine gun that the Commissariat had rejected two years previously. Degtyarev said, 'What are you young people up to?' Kalashnikov stood aside for his superior, who looked down at the parts of a dismantled rifle that were laid on the bench.

'What is this?' he asked.

'This is KBP-580, Sergeant Kalashnikov's prototype,' replied an official.

'Then put it together for us, sergeant,' said the general. 'Let us see it.'

Kalashnikov was well practised at assembling his own rifle, and put the weapon together in under two minutes. Degtyarev took the weapon from him and turned it over in his hands. It did not look like any of the other entries for the competition that he had seen. It was certainly not like Degtyarev's own design, which was in essence an adaptation of the carbine already in service with the Soviet army. The barrel of Kalashnikov's rifle was shorter than that of a standard carbine rifle but longer than that of a machine gun. It had a wooden stock and pistol-style handle, and a metal receiver with a simple lever device for selecting the automatic and semi-automatic firing modes. Below the lever there was a specially enlarged trigger guard—a clever touch, it allowed the gun to be fired without the operator taking his gloves off. In front of the trigger guard was a wooden handgrip from which emerged the gun's main barrel. Above the barrel there was what looked like a second barrel but was actually a tube that redirected the hot gas produced by firing, using the energy to propel the piston and fire the next round. The rounds were housed in an ammunition magazine that sat in front of the trigger guard and below the barrel, curving forwards and away from the trigger guard.

Degtyarev looked down the barrel. He moved his hand forward and clicked the fire selector up from single shot to automatic fire, grunting his amused approval. 'Your solution to the selector problem is certainly original.'

'Thank you, general,' replied a nervous Kalashnikov, not entirely sure if he was being reprimanded or complimented by the great man. Degtyarev ran his hand once more over the cold metal of the receiver and the roughly turned wood of the stock. Intrigued by the rifle's comparative lightness even with a fully loaded ammunition magazine, he balanced it on one hand for a moment and said nothing. Then, smiling for the first time that day, he turned again to the officials behind him.

'I do not think there is much sense in sending my prototypes to the tests. The design of the sergeant's prototype is better and more promising. You can see it with the naked eye.' The officials laughed nervously at the general's words. 'So, perhaps we will have to send my prototype to a museum. Good day, Comrade Kalashnikov.'

The general walked away laughing, the officials scurrying after him, leaving Kalashnikov with his mouth open and the other technicians in the room looking at him with barely concealed wonder.

When he had recovered his poise Kalashnikov turned back to his rifle. Suddenly it looked very small in comparison to the objectives it was supposed to meet. If Kalashnikov won the competition, his rifle would equip millions of troops in the Soviet armed forces for the next decade— it would be the weapon his country would use to maintain control of the vast swaths of territory it had acquired with victory in the Second World War and to defend that territory if war broke out with the United States. Such a war was at the forefront of Kalashnikov's mind. He knew that any conventional conflict with the Americans would be fought by mobile troops. Russian infantrymen would be taken into battle inside cramped armoured troop carriers, so they would need a shorter weapon. The armies would clash on the windswept heaths and in the ruined cities of Germany, where a successful rifle would be exposed to dust, damp and extremes of cold and heat yet still be required to provide accuracy over distance and a devastating rate of fire at close range. The gun must be easy to operate and clean. And as the troops who would carry it into battle would come from all of the Soviet Union's far-flung republics, speak a variety of languages and often be barely literate, it must be simple.

Did Kalashnikov have that weapon? The rate of fire was a fearsome 650 rounds per minute and, although the rifle kicked a little to the left when it was fired on full automatic, it had easily met the accuracy requirements of the contest. It was certainly simple enough; there were only eight moving parts. Could Degtyarev be right? Was his gun really good enough to win the competition? Kalashnikov was up against the elite of Soviet small arms designers—not just Degtyarev but other famous names such as Tokarev, Siminov, Shpagin, Bulkin and Dementyev. Fedor Tokarev had invented the standard semi-automatic side arm for Soviet forces, the TT pistol (the first T was for Tokarev and the second for Tula, where the weapon was designed and manufactured) and Georgii Shpagin could take credit for the PPSh41, the sub-machine gun that had done so much to win the war for the Soviet Union.

But the competition had been announced three years previously and, despite the calibre of the men who had entered, there was still no winner. And all the competitors, be they famous or relatively unknown, were obliged to meet the same exacting technical and performance criteria. If they were to be judged by their gun's toughness and performance, then Kalashnikov knew he stood a very good chance of success. KBP-580 had been immersed in water for an hour and dragged barrel-first through sand and mud; the mechanism had been soaked and the barrel clogged, and it had still fired without fail. Although Kalashnikov was not yet aware of it, the judges were astounded by the weapon's resilience and reliability and none of the other entries in the competition had performed so well. And he had another, vital, advantage: Kalashnikov was a war hero. But alongside the combat background that made him such an attractive figure to the propagandists there was another story, a story of intrigue and imprisonment and escape. Kalashnikov was undoubtedly a war hero— there was nothing invented about the remarkable calmness he had shown under fire or the wounds and shell-shock he had suffered—but he had also been an enemy of the state and a fugitive from Soviet justice. Kalashnikov had seen his family split apart, his father die and his brother's health broken on Stalin's whim. The genius of the man who would invent the AK47 and do so much to enforce the reign of communism around the world had actually been forged in opposition to the Soviet state. Kalashnikov might have died at the hands of the communists long before he faced the Nazis.

Mikhail Timofeyevich Kalashnikov was born on 10 November 1919 in the village of Kurya, on the wide steppes of south-western Siberia's Altai territory close to the border with Kazakhstan. There were two sisters and six brothers in the family, of which Mysha, as he was known, was the second oldest. The family were kulaks, peasants who owned a farmstead with basic agricultural machinery and enough land to produce a small surplus to trade. Although they were not impoverished—indeed, kulaks were regarded in some quarters as wealthy—it was a precarious existence that depended upon the vagaries of nature and relentless hard work. Money was jealously guarded or reinvested in the farm, and any piece of machinery that broke was repaired on the spot or its parts recycled. Like everyone else, young Mysha was obliged to help. The boy was fascinated by the way machinery worked, and by the time he was ten he had a thorough understanding of mechanics. Seventy-five years later Kalashnikov remembered: 'I learned to be an artisan in the farmyard. That is why I have some understanding, even now, of the men in the small workshops who make pirate AKs in Pakistan and the Middle East. That takes great skill and I learned to work and design in a similar way to how I am sure they did, fixing things because you could not afford to waste anything.'

In this diligent way the Kalashnikovs managed to survive from year to year, riding out the storms of civil war and famine that blew across the land in the wake of the 1917 Revolution. But many of their neighbours were less successful, and as Bolshevik rule established itself across the country the family attracted the envy and enmity of landless villagers. Mysha was as oblivious to this creeping resentment as he was to the traumatic attempts of first Lenin and then Stalin to reorganize peasant life along communist lines. All he knew was hard work and the occasional excitement of hunting trips when he was allowed to carry his father's rifle as the village men tracked elk and deer in the forest. On good hunts they would return with enough food to last a month if the meat was eked out in stews and the stock used to make soups. In this time-honoured way the family got by. Kalashnikov's older sisters, Nyura and Gasha, were married off, new livestock was bought, the fields were sown and the harvests were gathered.

But while Mysha was learning to repair broken axles and springs on the farm, far away in Moscow orders were being given that would end his peasant life on the Altai. In 1928 Stalin launched the first Five Year Plan, a drive to enforce rapid and massive industrialization throughout the Soviet Union. Entire new manufacturing centres were hurriedly thrown up—cities containing hundreds of thousands of workers who had to be fed. To achieve this, Stalin decreed that food production also be put on an industrial footing and the nation's agricultural system collectivized. Across the Soviet Union peasants such as Mysha's family, with a little land of their own, resisted the ensuing attempts to herd them into communal farms and, rather than accept the fixed prices that the state now offered for their crops and livestock, they killed their cows and pigs and burnt their wheat. In the Altai region troops were deployed to put down resistance, and when agricultural production fell disastrously across the entire country Stalin blamed peasant intransigence rather than a plan that attacked one of the few parts of the Soviet economy that worked.

In early 1932 the Kalashnikovs were denounced by a Communist Party official in the village. At first this meant nothing more serious than some name calling: Mysha continued to walk down the village street to school as usual, only now the boys from the poorer families would yell 'Kulak!' as he passed. The young lad, who had no clear idea what the difference between a kulak and a comrade was, would happily chase them off. But over the months the atmosphere in the village changed. The police, who had previously been friendly, became terse and aggressive, the taunting on the way to school changed from name calling to stone throwing, and Mysha started to get into regular fights. One evening, after a fight had caused a crowd to gather, their father told Mysha and his brothers that from now on they were to ignore any taunts and do nothing that could give the authorities an excuse to arrest them. Pushed and jeered on his way to and from school, Mysha now cried with frustration but did not fight back. His father buried himself in his work, hoping the family could survive until the authorities came to their senses and allowed them to get on with farming as they had always done.

It didn't happen. Instead, Stalin called for the 'liquidation of the kulaks as a class' and unleashed a frenzied attack against the peasants who produced the bulk of the country's food. The attack was as wide-ranging as it was illogical: the Soviet Union's own archive figures estimate that 5 million people were deported to Siberia and other penal regions, and hundreds of thousands were shot or died in the prison camps as the Soviet Union descended into a collective madness. The terror reached the Kalashnikovs on an autumn morning in 1932. Mysha's eldest brother Victor had gone into hiding, but the rest of the family were at home when a mob burst through the farm gates driving the family's livestock into the snow-covered yard. The air was filled with a terrified lowing and bleating. From the window Mysha watched as the men pulled long knives from their belts and slaughtered all the animals. An hour later all that remained was a pile of entrails and the mob had moved on to the outbuildings, which they began to strip of machinery.

Convinced that the men would come for the family next, Mysha stood petrified behind the windows until he heard the clatter of hooves and a squad of mounted police arrived at the farmhouse door. But they had not come to disperse the crowd; they had come to disperse the Kalashnikovs. The family were ordered to take what pots and bedding they could carry and were then bundled on to two horse-drawn sleds. After a bewildered and freezing two-hour journey to the nearest railway yard they were pushed on to a cattle truck with two other kulak families and one bucket to serve as sanitation for eighteen people.

Three days later the train pulled into a siding at Nizhnyaya Mokhovaya, a penal colony in the Bakchar region of Siberia, 800 kilometres east of the Altai. Guards pulled the sliding doors back and banged on the side of the carriages with the stocks of their rifles. As the doors opened a harsh, blinding winter light poured into the fetid space and it took Mysha a minute or so to focus on what was happening outside. All along the train people were being pushed out and jumping down to the ground. The guards forced the deportees into ranks and then ran along the lines of confused families barking out orders, their carbine rifles swinging on their shoulders. Mysha had never seen so many soldiers at the same time, or so many guns. He merged into the crowd, herded at gunpoint until hundreds of men, women and children stood before a commissar who spat his contempt at them: 'You are not comrades now. You are inhabitants of a penal colony—that means you are here to be punished. Work hard, colonists, and maybe one day you will be comrades again.'

The family had been fortunate not to have been shot like thousands of others, but deportation was nevertheless a disaster for them. Victor had been caught by the police and, after a brief appearance before a tribunal in Kurya, was sentenced to nine years' hard labour (when he was released seven years later and asked, 'Why am I being released?' he was promptly reimprisoned for asking questions, so when he was released again two years afterwards he said nothing). At the end of their first winter in Nizhnyaya Mokhovaya Mysha's father died of exhaustion. His mother remarried the next year, so now Mysha was crammed into a cottage with not only his own family but a new father and step-siblings. As a result he spent as much time as he could hunting in the woods with an ancient rifle until in 1935, at the age of fifteen, he simply walked out of the colony and went home.

Concealing himself in ditches and woods to avoid militia patrols with orders to shoot escapees, it took him seven days to reach Taiga railway station. There he was able to catch a train to Pospelika, only 65 kilometres short of Kurya; a distance he covered in a day on foot. Collapsing at the door of his sister Nyura's house, he rested for two weeks before finding work as a lumberjack on a collective farm. The physical labour soon proved too strenuous for his weakened muscles. Rather than be a burden on Nyura, he moved in with his eldest sister, Gasha. Her husband was a party official and treated Mysha as a contemptible 'kulak'. Worse, when Mysha visited what had been his family home he found it had been burned to the ground. Defeated and dismayed Mysha took a parcel of bread from Nyura and returned to Nizhnaya Mokhovaya. After begging rides from passing trucks, walking for days at a time, and suffering from fever on the way, Mysha finally returned, three months after he had set off.

The trip had been an attempt to recapture his past but its effect had been the opposite—Kalashnikov had discovered his future. He had set off as a boy called Mysha who wanted to rediscover the comforts and certainties of childhood, but he came back as Mikhail, a man who knew that the only way he could prosper and survive was by his own efforts. He had shown enough bravery and single-minded purpose to suggest that he could set his mind to anything and succeed. And increasingly Kalashnikov was turning his mind to guns, stripping the local men's rifles for the pleasure of seeing how they were constructed. People in Nizhnaya Mokhovaya said Kalashnikov was 'crazy' about guns, but there was no apparent harm in his obsession and they took advantage of his willingness to mend any machinery that was brought to him. And then in 1936 Kalashnikov's close friend Gavril Bondarenko, a nineteen-year-old accounts clerk on a nearby collective farm who had also been exiled from Kurya, gave him an incredible gift—an American Browning pistol.

Where Bondarenko had got hold of such rare and dangerous treasure is unclear. Over seventy years after the event Kalashnikov can no longer remember or will not say, but whatever its provenance the Browning was priceless to him. In the secrecy of the woods he reverently cleaned and dismantled the pistol. All the previous guns he had taken to pieces had been bolt-action carbines, rifles that need to be loaded for each shot. The Browning was a semi-automatic: looking inside its intricate and delicate mechanism Kalashnikov discovered a whole new world. It was, he remembers, 'a thing of wonder'.

In Nizhnyaya Mokhovaya good relations with the authorities could be the difference between survival and disaster. If the police stopped a member of a family working, or arrested the main breadwinner, hunger would follow quickly for the rest of the family. They would turn a blind eyed to the smuggling of contraband goods as long as they were kept happy and nothing happened that drew attention to the arrangement. A gun, however, was different, and when word reached them of a deportee possessing an unregistered and illegal semi-automatic weapon they came for Kalashnikov. After hammering with the butts of their rifles against the cottage door until his mother let them in they stripped the house—but found nothing, for Kalashnikov had hidden the Browning in a nearby woodpile. He was handcuffed and taken to the village jail. If Kalashnikov had revealed where he had hidden the gun he could have been shot or pitched into the dark maze of the gulags, but the teenager held his nerve and stayed silent.

Exasperated, the militia released him, hoping he would lead them to the gun's hiding place. Kalashnikov decided to walk out of the penal colony again, but this time he would be a criminal fugitive rather than simply a boy trying to recapture his lost childhood. Four days after he had been arrested Kalashnikov retrieved the Browning and went to the collective farm where Bondarenko waited for him with forged papers. The pair walked for three weeks until one morning in May 1937 they limped into the Kazakhstan-Siberian railway yards in Alma-Ata where Bondarenko's uncle worked.

Kalashnikov was taken on as an apprentice at the engineers' yard, which employed thousands of men not just to build the railways but also to maintain the track and the rolling stock. It was an academy of excellence where the young man would add industrial knowledge and technical know-how to his peasant mechanic's skills. The yard was also a vital part of the Soviet industrialization drive and subject to strict security measures. Although it was a good place to disappear, it was a bad place to be known as a fugitive from a penal colony. After completing his two-year railway engineer's apprenticeship Kalashnikov was promoted to technical clerk. None of his workmates knew anything of his desperate escape, just as it would remain a secret when he joined the factory's branch of the Communist Party—the institution that had, until recently, being trying to imprison or kill him. 'Of course it would have told upon my relations with the authorities,' Kalashnikov would later admit. 'They would have found many things in my revelations, which, from their highly ideological point of view, would have been a barrier to me becoming what I am now. Who would have allowed me to work in such a secret domain as weapons?'

Soviet society was itself a secret domain, illogical and governed by terror, but some sections of society were important enough to be left relatively unmolested—very few designers were incarcerated and none were shot. As Kalashnikov served his apprenticeship in Alma-Ata men such as Degtyarev, Tokarev and their comrades were being left alone to work on a process that had begun twenty-five years previously during the reign of the last tsar, Nicholas II: the search for an effective and accurate assault rifle.

In the First World War infantrymen carrying carbines and walking towards heavy machine guns had been slaughtered in the hundreds of thousands. Russian infantrymen on the Eastern Front had carried the Mosin-Nagant, a carbine that required the rifle's bolt to be pulled back to reload after each shot. It was no match for the fixed automatic weapons that dominated no man's land, and its length was a handicap when troops were fighting in narrow trenches. The rifle was accurate, but in close combat it is rapid rate of fire rather than accuracy that decides the outcome and in 1916 Vladimir Gregory Fedorov, the court weapons designer, unveiled a semi-automatic weapon that appeared to offer that rate of fire: the Fedorov Avtomat self-loading rifle.

At that time the central problem for designers of semi-automatic and automatic rifles was the calibre of the ammunition. Russia's standard 7.62 x 54mm rifle cartridge was too heavy for delicate early self-loading firing mechanisms, but the smaller cartridges used by pistols and sub-machine guns lacked the power that guaranteed a soldier a kill if he hit his target. Fedorov made many attempts to design his gun around the 7.62 x 54 but he was continually thwarted by the damage the cartridge did to the firing mechanism, causing it to wear out and misfire. Fedorov found an answer by sacrificing power and adapting his gun to fire the smaller Japanese

6.5mm Meiji 30 cartridge.

The Fedorov Avtomat had a single shot and semi-automatic mode and, although its effectiveness was limited by its small twenty-five-round ammunition magazine, it can justifiably be seen as the world's first assault rifle—a weapon that could turn an infantryman reliant on his comrades' rate of fire into an individual killing machine. If Fedorov's revolutionary rifle had been manufactured in great numbers it could have changed the fortunes of Imperial Russia's war against Germany and Austro-Hungary. But the innovation came too late to stop Russia's enforced withdrawal from the war or to save Tsar Nicholas II. The Bolsheviks who seized power in 1917 were distrustful of a designer who had been so closely associated with the court and Fedorov was imprisoned. He was released after two months but even in 1920, at the height of the civil war between the Bolsheviks and the Whites and their Western supporters, production of the Avtomat failed to rise above a desultory fifty a week. In 1924 manufacture of the Fedorov Avtomat ceased altogether. Unbowed, Fedorov returned to the search for an intermediate cartridge alongside Soviet designers such as Fedor Tokarev and Vasily Degtyarev.

The Germans, too, had learned the lessons of the First World War, and by 1935 they had developed the 7.75mm intermediate round and the semi-automatic MKb 35 rifle. Three years later Tokarev had produced two automatic rifles, the SVT38 and SVT40. None of these weapons was a fully functional assault rifle: the MKb 35 was extremely fragile and also inaccurate, and the Tokarev weapons were essentially carbines with a semi-automatic mode. They were sub-machine guns—automatic weapons with very high rates of fire that used pistol bullets but lacked the range and power of an assault rifle—and as such would have been available to the Soviet army but for the fact that Stalin personally intervened in 1939 to ensure that more carbines than sub-machine guns came out of the arms factories: rifles were cheaper and quicker to manufacture. Even so, when Russia next went to war against Germany in 1941 there were often not enough carbines to go round and Soviet troops were often forced to share their weapons. As far as small arms were concerned, Russia would enter the conflict with Nazi Germany under-equipped and technically disadvantaged.

Consequently, when twenty-two-year-old Red Army sergeant Mikhail Kalashnikov stood up in the turret of his T-34 tank in early September that year and listened to the unmistakable rattle and creak of Mark IV Panzers approaching through the woods, many of the soldiers around him were so badly armed that they had little chance of survival against German infantry. He was already drawing the obvious conclusion: 'I saw some of our soldiers were sharing a rifle between three men. What chance could we have when our own men were extremely brave but badly equipped? From those early days of the war I knew that the answer was to design guns that were reliable and simple enough to manufacture in great numbers. We needed millions of such guns.'

Kalashnikov had been called up in 1938, and his technical ability had quickly been recognized. He had designed a tank shell counter that allowed crews to keep an automatic tally of their shots in battle—vital information when a tank duel could be decided by knowing which of the opposing crews had a shell remaining in its gun barrel—and a device that enabled tank commanders to fire their TT pistols from the hatch-down turret of a T-34. In June 1941 Kalashnikov won an army competition to design a device to measure tank engine performance and was personally congratulated by Marshal Zhukov, the man whose military leadership would eventually bring about the defeat of Hitler's ambitions in the East. 'I was only a sergeant and here I was meeting Zhukov,' Kalashnikov remembers. 'It was like meeting a god. You can't imagine what it was like for me.' Recognizing Kalashnikov's unique abilities, Zhukov had the tank commander posted to Leningrad to work on further technical developments.

It was not to be a long posting. On 22 June 1941 Hitler launched Operation Barbarossa, a massive blitzkrieg across the borders of the Soviet Union with the objective of wiping the communist state from the face of the earth. Hitler came close to succeeding: within the first week of Barbarossa the Russians suffered 150,000 dead and wounded, a scale of loss comparable to the slaughter of the First World War. Hundreds of thousands of Russian troops were cut off and then destroyed by lightning pincer movements from German armoured divisions.

Stunned by the initial hammer blow of Barbarossa, the Red Army struggled to extract itself from encirclement. The Russian tactics were to blunt the shock of the German attacks and rescue as many cut-off units as possible. Kalashnikov was made a platoon commander in early September, and over seventy years later he was still staggered at the chaos they were thrown into: 'We didn't know where we were, in the enemy's rear or at the front line. Our life was made up of endless marches, short and vicious strikes at the enemy's flanks; it seemed we were always attempting to break through to infantry units that had been cut off by the speed of the German advance.' In this fast-changing and confused situation German tanks would lunge unexpectedly out of areas that were supposed to be held by the Red Army. When attempting to retreat, Kalashnikov would find himself accidentally advancing towards the enemy because the Germans had encircled the Soviet positions. But now, at last, on this early autumn morning Kalashnikov was attacking the enemy whom he could hear crawling towards him.

He gripped the side of the turret with one hand, checked that the mouthpiece of his intercom was correctly in place with the other, and prepared to give the order to advance. It was an unseasonably cold morning but Kalashnikov's hands were already wet with sweat. Around his T-34 Soviet infantrymen hurried to their strongpoints or crouched down behind birch trees, laughably fragile figures in the face of the approaching onslaught. Kalashnikov kept his eyes fixed straight ahead and wedged his spine against the steel back support, bracing his body against the lurch that sudden advance would send through the tank's hull.

Kalashnikov's was one of five Soviet tanks hunkered down in ambush behind a low rise on the side of a wooded escarpment that faced south-west. Sixteen kilometres behind him lay the city of Bryansk and a further 300 kilometres behind that the Russian capital, Moscow. Directly ahead of Kalashnikov was the German army. The Panzers he could hear through the autumn mist were the spearhead of a force of one million men, 1700 tanks, 19,500 artillery guns and 950 combat aircraft that Adolf Hitler had personally instructed to take Moscow before winter brought the 1941 offensive to a halt. The Russian high command, Stavka, had ordered that the Germans were to be held along a line outside Bryansk while Zhukov prepared the defence of the capital. The Russians did not expect victory— no German blitzkrieg attack had yet been successfully resisted anywhere. The realistic objective was to hold the Germans long enough for winter and Zhukov to make Moscow impregnable.

The steel hull offered the tanks protection against much of the incoming fire, and crews could even survive a direct hit from a German shell. But infantrymen caught out in the open were terribly exposed and Kalashnikov had seen scores of troops killed or injured by mechanized German attacks that literally tore through the Russian lines. Many times he had seen recklessly brave resistance by Red Army infantry break down because Soviet troops were unable to put down enough fire on the battlefield. As eight German tanks began to move up the slope towards the Russian infantry positions Kalashnikov wondered if he was about to see the same situation play out again. 'We were just inside the edge of the forest and we could only wait as the tanks approached. I was desperate not to give our position away.'

Two weeks earlier, Kalashnikov had done just that. While waiting in ambush he had accidentally leaned against the heavy machine gun mounted on the tank's turret. The gun went off, raking the birch trees and bushes round about with tracer fire that splintered the trunks and shook the foliage until it flashed, giving away their position to anyone within a kilometre or so. Kalashnikov's driver slammed the gears into reverse and the T-34 smashed out of the thicket seconds before a barrage of German shells crashed down and obliterated their position. This time Kalashnikov kept well away from the gun.

'The Germans were coming closer to our positions all the time and I was sure that they must see us in the trees. I knew we must keep our nerves under control because there was really no other way to do it. If you want to destroy Panzers then you have to take them completely by surprise, and in that moment—when they are still shocked to find that you are there—you must out-manoeuvre them and get around the back. All tanks, even the best in the world, are vulnerable to attack from the back because the heaviest armour plating is on the front. So I knew what had to be done, but some of the crew found the tension very hard to take—they wanted to attack. I watched the line of Panzers until they were nearly at the top of the hill and on to the positions that our troops were manning in front of the trees. If they had got on top of the infantry there would be slaughter. My driver lost his patience and yelled out, "Why are we not moving, commander? They are going to crush our infantry!"

'Then finally the attack message came. As our tank pulled out of the woods the first thing I saw was the ground in front of us; it was terribly churned up by caterpillar tracks. This infuriated me because they were the ruts that we had made on our retreating the week before—they were a sign of defeat and panic. We dashed onwards firing, and as we advanced I saw German tanks begin to burn. The German infantry tried to run around them but we had cut them off—they were trapped and our machine guns cut them down.'

The Germans threw more tanks into the battle, and in their turn attacked the Russian rear. Having lost the advantage of their superior position the leading Russian tank attempted to escape the onslaught, and Kalashnikov's tank followed. 'Enemy shells began to fall all around us, but we managed to keep following the commander's tank and disappeared into a gully at the back of the hill. Not only had we got away from them but we had come around the enemy's flank, so now the German tanks were obliged to follow us—it was like a merry-go-round! One by one by one we knocked out the enemy tanks until finally we had beaten their attack.' It was a rare success, and when the fighting had finished the churned up ground showed the price paid by the Russian infantry to gain it. Dozens of dead and injured lay amongst the ruts.

As September wore bloodily on the Germans gradually overwhelmed the Russian resistance outside Bryansk, and eventually Kalashnikov's tank was hit during another counter-attack. 'We were trying to get around the flanks of the enemy, but this time they were ready for the manoeuvre and we drove straight into the range of an artillery battery.' A thunderous storm of incoming artillery fire landed around the Russian tanks, but before Kalashnikov could successfully bring his own guns to bear on an enemy target a Panzer shell slammed into the side of the T-34. Kalashnikov, who was standing upright in the turret with the hatch open, saw his commander's tank burst into flames in front of him and was then himself engulfed by blinding white light and overpowering noise.

Miraculously the shell did not pierce the armour plating and incinerate everyone within the vehicle, but as his vision cleared Kalashnikov looked down and, seeing only smoke and blood, immediately feared the worst for his crew. He shouted down to them through the acrid fumes, and one by one his crew replied, 'Here, sergeant!...I'm fine.' It was only then that Kalashnikov realized the blood on his overalls was his own, and he fainted. 'The pain was immense. A piece of armour had been dislodged from the tank by the impact of the shell and passed through my shoulder. I don't know how long I was unconscious, but when I came round we had disengaged the enemy. Someone was undoing my overalls. I felt as if my shoulder and arms belonged to somebody else.'

Kalashnikov was loaded on to an ambulance truck with a doctor and nurse and eleven other injured men for evacuation to a field hospital. He began to hallucinate, but even in lucid moments it seemed to him as he looked out between the canvas flaps at the back of the moving truck that his army had simply disappeared. It was not Kalashnikov's imagination: as pain gradually brought him back to full consciousness he realized that the Russians had abandoned this sector. But had the German advance encircled their section of the front line?

Of the twelve injured men, only Kalashnikov and a lieutenant with burnt hands were able to walk unaided, and at the end of the first day they went ahead with the driver to reconnoitre a village in the hope of finding safe shelter. Their only weapons were the driver's Mosin-Nagant and Kalashnikov's TT pistol. This would not be enough to fight off Germans with automatic weapons, and they approached the main street with extreme caution. Suddenly a burst of automatic fire came down the road, splintering stones and throwing up dirt and dust. The three men dashed for cover and then crawled back into the woods on the edge of the village. Struggling to get their breath back, they heard more automatic fire coming from the direction of their truck. Running through the trees, they reached the vehicle in time to see the back of a German motorbike patrol pulling round the corner. The ambulance engine was on fire and the nurse and the doctor lay dead in the road. Inside the truck there was an inch of blood under the bullet-torn corpses of the other men. The lieutenant and then Kalashnikov vomited in the road. The driver cried.

'If we had one automatic weapon,' said the lieutenant, 'we could have stopped this.'

Kalashnikov nodded and added, 'But we don't.'

The three men waited in the woods until night fell and then set off towards the east in search of the Soviet lines. But the front was even more fluid than the disoriented men had realized, and after tramping through dense woodland they encountered a terrified peasant who told them they were now deep in the occupied zone. The driver was not a medic and Kalashnikov and the lieutenant were both badly in need of treatment, so the peasant directed them to the house of Nikolai Ivanovich, the local healer. Delirious, dehydrated and suffering almost unbearable pain from his shoulder wound Kalashnikov staggered along with his two comrades, drifting in and out of consciousness. When his eyes were open images of the slaughter by the roadside flashed across his vision as if he was walking through a nightmare. The house was only sixteen kilometres away, but it took the party two nights to cover the distance. The Germans had already threatened to hang the healer but he hid the men in his small barn, treated their wounds as best he could and fed them from his meagre stock of apples, bread and potatoes. Badly wounded and shell-shocked as he was, Kalashnikov's spirits sank. 'I wondered if we would get out of there— would I survive the terrible slaughter and see my family again? I was in great pain and it didn't look like we had much hope. But then, during the war we all had a different spirit—we stuck together and we were capable of doing incredible things.'

Along with the food the healer brought back reports of the fighting. It was not good news: all across the front the Germans were advancing. The men were determined to get back to their own side—wherever that might be now. By their third evening in the barn Kalashnikov had recovered enough strength to attempt to set out again, and after Ivanovich had dressed the men's wounds for the last time he led them through the dark vegetable plots to the edge of the village. Still only armed with a pistol and one carbine they continued their journey as they had begun it, hiding by day and walking by night.

Within three days the rations had run out. Luckily, since it was autumn, there were still a few berries on the bushes and mushrooms under the trees. But after five days they found no more food and were forced to eat grass. When desperation forced them to drink swamp water they suffered terrible stomach cramps and vomiting. Kalashnikov was virtually in a coma when, seven days after they had left Ivanovich's barn, the men staggered into the Russian forward positions. As he was stretchered into an ambulance Kalashnikov made a decision: 'I couldn't get the sound of the German automatic out of my head. I decided then that I would invent a gun. My comrades needed a weapon that would allow them to fight back.'

Over the next two months as he lay in his hospital bed deep in the East Kalashnikov read the standard work on automatic weapons, Fedorov's *Evolution of Small Arms*, from cover to cover, contemplating its emphasis on the necessity of an intermediate round. Once he was able to walk around the ward he sat on the edge of wounded men's beds and asked them to describe their ideal infantry rifle. What would it look like? How would it perform? What exactly did they want in a gun? Was it killing power? Range? Lightness? Durability? Ease of use?

As Kalashnikov was working towards his own conception of an assault rifle the Soviet army was increasingly being armed with a simple and effective automatic gun. Dismayed by the initial German successes in late 1941 Stalin allowed mass production of Georgii Shpagin's PPSh41 machine gun to go ahead, and by spring 1942 hundreds of thousands of these new weapons were reaching Soviet front-line troops. The PPSh41 was not an assault rifle, but its designer had created a sub-machine gun that delivered the 7.62 x 25mm pistol round at a rate of 900 rounds per minute. All the gun's metal parts were stamped, so the body had no screws or bolts, and the grips were made from roughly machined wood. It was extremely robust and, although it did not have the range of accuracy or power of an assault rifle, it was manufactured in such large numbers that the Soviet infantry were able to deliver devastating amounts of automatic fire in close-quarter fighting. Over 6 million PPSh41s were produced, an indicator of the extraordinary scale and speed of Soviet industrial production. Within a year of the shock and near disaster of Barbarossa the Soviet armaments industry, relocated to the East and out of range of enemy bombing raids, was producing more arms, munitions and material than the Germans.

In this great move eastward one figure had passed relatively unnoticed. When Kalashnikov was discharged from hospital he was still so shell-shocked that he was given six months' leave to recover. He took a train to Kazakhstan and returned to the Alma-Ata engineers' yard where he had served his apprenticeship. Aware that the immediate need now was for machine guns, he asked his old bosses for workbench room and sat down with an ex-workmate called Zhenya Kravchenko, a skilled metal machinist, to make a successor to the PPSh41.

Throughout the winter of 1942–3 Kalashnikov worked on the prototype, and after six months he had the gun that he now remembers as 'black lacquered machine gun number one'. It was triumph enough to produce a working automatic weapon in such circumstances, but Kalashnikov's next move displayed an almost reckless self-confidence. He presented himself and his machine gun at the Kazakhstan regional military headquarters at Alma-Ata and asked the gate officer to inform the military commissar that Sergeant Kalashnikov had arrived. Faced with an unauthorized weapon and the unheard-of demand from a sergeant to speak to a military commissar, the officer immediately presumed the worst and threw Kalashnikov in the guardhouse. No one at headquarters knew who he was, and his performance at the gate could easily be taken as that of an assassin or saboteur. After three days in which no one believed his story, execution became increasingly likely.

But he was no longer Kalashnikov the fugitive; this was Kalashnikov the party member and the man who had been personally recommended by Marshal Zhukov, and old connections came to his rescue. A comrade from the railway yards branch of the party now worked as an assistant to the Central Committee of the Kazakhstan Communist Party, and Kalashnikov persuaded a released prisoner to take a message to him. The outcome was his own immediate release. 'I was lucky to have friends,' Kalashnikov later recalled with some understatement. 'There was an atmosphere of secrecy then, and you could pay dearly for mistakes.' The same connections got Kalashnikov access to Vasily Kaishigulov, Secretary of the Central Committee of the Kazakhstan Communist Party and the man in charge of Kazakhstan's defence industry. Kaishigulov was impressed enough by 'machine gun number one' to find Kalashnikov a place at one of the Soviet Union's main arms development centres, the Moscow Aviation Institute, which had been evacuated to Kazakhstan for the duration of the war.

Now Kalashnikov's progress became rapid. From the Aviation Institute Kalashnikov was sent to the Dzerzhinsky Ordnance Academy, where A. A. Blagonravov was the head of weapons development. Blagonravov, the most famous weapons scientist in the Soviet Union and an immensely influential figure in the Soviet arms industry, rejected Kalashnikov's machine gun number one as offering no real improvement on the PPSh41 but recognized that the newcomer's clear-headed approach to complex technical problems marked him out as a potentially great designer. Blagonravov personally endorsed Kalashnikov's 'exceptional ability' and recommended that he be attached to the Red Army's Main Ordnance Directorate. This put Kalashnikov at the very heart of the Russian weapons programme in 1943. In the same year Zhukov won the battle of Kursk, where 2700 Panzers smashed against 3600 Soviet tanks in the biggest armoured encounter the world would ever see.

After Kursk the Russians steadily pushed the Axis forces back towards Berlin, but this progress was regularly held up by enemy soldiers carrying a new weapon. The German MKb 35mm had the same problems as all previous assault rifles: wear and tear on the mechanism caused it to misfire and jam. Nazi engineers responded with the Kurz 7.9mm intermediate round and a remodelled and upgraded rifle to fire it, the MP43. However, Hitler was slower than Stalin to appreciate the great advantages that a semi-automatic rifle would offer his troops, and he cancelled further development and production of the weapon in the face of the Reich's increasing supply and logistics problems following the defeat at Kursk. But German generals on the Eastern Front insisted on more supplies of a weapon that was able to hold back masses of Russian infantry armed with Shpagin's gun, and, like Stalin before him, Hitler changed his mind. The MP43 was upgraded and renamed the StG44, for *Sturmgewehr 1944*; and *Sturmgewehr* translates as storm, or assault, rifle.

The new German rifle had a sloped ammunition magazine, was gas-powered and boasted a rate of fire of 500 rounds per minute. Like the Fedorov Avtomat the StG44 came too late to save the regime that created it, but the Nazis made a very serious effort to produce the weapon in large numbers. By the end of the war, 425,977 MP43s and derivatives had been manufactured, the bulk of which were deployed on the Eastern Front. But Kalashnikov still insists, 'I didn't see captured German weapons. They were top-secret. I was just a sergeant. How could I get access to them?' Perhaps Kalashnikov did not see an MP43—although it seems unlikely that the major Russian weapons research and development centres in which he worked did not have supplies of German weaponry for their designer technician to test. A captured StG44 was demonstrated at a meeting of the Soviet Arms Committee in 1943, and within six months two military engineers, Nikolay Elizarov and Pavel Ryazanov, had produced the 7.62 x 39mm cartridge. It was this intermediate cartridge that made Fedorov's dreams of a Russian assault rifle a reality; it only required someone to design the dream. In the autumn of 1943 the People's Commissariat on

Armaments announced the competition to find that person.

Kalashnikov was not amongst the favourites. His 'machine gun number one' had been rejected and there were other, much bigger, names chasing the prize. But his work had enabled him to master automatic firing mechanisms, and his combat experience and the long hours spent talking to wounded men in hospital had given him an in-depth knowledge of what Soviet soldiers wanted from their rifles. Working quietly with engineers Sasha Zaitsev and Vladimir Deikin, Kalashnikov set about the task.

The technician in charge of testing at Kovrov was Vasily Lyuty, one of the men who had rejected Kalashnikov's machine gun; but he held the young designer in high enough regard to follow his progress closely, making suggestions at each stage of the rifle's development. Kalashnikov was not innately a better designer than the other men already working on the project, but he possessed an individual will that was greater than theirs and an unerring ability to see a simple solution to a complex problem. Long after the Kovrov workshops had closed for the night the light would still be on above Kalashnikov's workbench and drawing board, and when the workshop opened again in the morning no one would be there before Kalashnikov: for two years he pushed himself relentlessly.

Although there are obvious exterior design similarities between the German assault rifle and the AK47, the interiors are very different. Perhaps looking back to his time in the woods with the Browning pistol that nearly cost him his life, Kalashnikov designed a firing mechanism that owed more to US than to German technology—it bears a closer resemblance to that of the American M1 rifle than to the StG44. Kalashnikov's over-riding criteria were simplicity and sturdiness. None of the parts was engineered to the ultimate degree; instead there was a built-in latitude that allowed the gun to withstand very rough treatment and still fire safely and accurately. As with fixing machines on the family farm this was about economy, in both use and expense—the rifle would last longer but would need cleaning less often. The gas piston was bigger than usual and the interior of the barrel, the firing chamber, and the gas piston and gas cylinder, were chromium-plated. This extended their working life by years and established the format that many weapons would follow in the future.

With patience and hard work Kalashnikov started to achieve very promising results. As he did so, other competitors began to drop away. In August 1946 Sudayev died suddenly at the age of thirty-three. Shortly afterwards Shpagin admitted that he had been unsuccessful in making the leap to the new cartridge and dropped out. Later in the same year Degtyarev, grey and beaten, informed the People's Commissariat that there had been 'too many stoppages' during the intense testing of his rifle. His ominous words came true, and his prototype was placed in a military museum. By January 1947 only Bulkin, Dementyev and Kalashnikov were left in the competition. Then Bulkin, whose infamous temper and disrespect for officials had never helped his cause, was eliminated.

The contest became a head-to-head between Kalashnikov and Dementyev, and the last week of the competition was the most extreme. Kalashnikov and Dementyev's rifles were dropped from heights, thrown in tanks of water and covered in mud, but still they both worked. On the last day the two rifles were given one more sand bath. Both were dipped in water and then immersed in a pit until every opening or crevice was crammed with grit. Then the rifles were taken to the firing range for the final time. Dementyev's rifle was tested first in single-shot mode. After three shots it misfired on the fourth and refused to fire again. Then came KBP-580. Kalashnikov held his breath as the tester moved the selector to single shot and fired. Sand flew out of the barrel and so did a bullet, which found its mark on the target. The tester fired three more shots, each time successfully, then pushed the fire selector to automatic and emptied the magazine without a single misfire. The words of the People's Commissariat on Armaments a week later were prosaic, but their implications enormous. 'The 7.62 assault rifle designed by senior sergeant Mikhail Kalashnikov is recommended to be fielded.'

Miraculously tough, artfully simple and devastating effective, Kalashnikov's invention would revolutionize the way guns were used on the battlefield and within fifty years change the world itself. It would defend the power of communist Russia and defeat capitalist America. It would become a signifier of international revolution, and yet its first international action would be to smash a people's revolution in Hungary in 1956. More immediately, the Soviets quickly established the creation myth of the AK47 as the gun designed by a heroic but pragmatic tank commander whose reliance and ingenuity first overcame bestial fascism with communist ingenuity and then solved the problem of the assault rifle. The Soviets didn't take their gun from the Nazis—what they actually took was the ammunition. But whether the AK47's true origins were ultimately peasant genius, communist industry or Nazi innovation, the gun was already spinning out its own mythology.

After the Second World War the USSR and the USA had both expected their next conflict to be against each other, and designed their weapons accordingly. Although their military technologies had clashed during the Korean War of 1950–3 it was not until the war in Vietnam that their respective assault rifles came up against each other in large-scale and protracted hostilities. The American military had adopted Eugene Stoner's M16 assault rifle to face the AK47 across the central German plain. Then in 1962 President Kennedy authorised unofficial American military involvement in Vietnam, where guerrilla warfare by the communist North against the pro-Western South had been steadily increasing since the post-colonial partition of the country in 1954, and was felt to be destabilizing the region. At this point it occurred to the US army that the M16 might not be at home in the rainforests of south-east Asia. The Department of Defence tested the weapon in jungle conditions and found problems with reliability and accuracy, but by then it was too late and the American GI was saddled with a gun that either misfired or failed to fire.

Communist China first supplied North Vietnam with Kalashnikovs in 1963, the year after the US military presence was established in South Vietnam. Within two years American troops began to speak in awe of the weapon used by their opponents and the failures of their own, supposedly more advanced, M16. By 1965 American officers were complaining of losing men because of weapon malfunction. In 1967 letters appeared in the *Washington Post*, and the performance of the M16 attracted the attention of the growing anti-war movement in the USA. As the M16's reputation diminished the AK47's grew stronger; GIs were dropping their M16s and picking up the AKs of dead Viet Cong troops. On several occasions this led to death by friendly fire when American units opened up on what they believed to be enemy positions because of the pop-pop-pop sound coming through the foliage. Throughout the 1960s Communist China gave hundreds of thousands of Norinco model 56 Kalashnikovs to the North Vietnamese. From the North the weapons were carried by porters or loaded on to bicycles and taken down the Ho Chi Minh Trail to supply insurgents in the American-controlled South.

Speed and camouflage were the Viet Cong's greatest strengths in jungle warfare, and equipment was kept to a bare minimum. While GIs would pour fully automatic M16 fire into a suspected enemy position, Viet Cong troops would fire short controlled bursts of semi-automatic fire from their Kalashnikovs. Typically, each guerrilla would carry only two hundred rounds of ammunition and would only open fire when he had an individual American soldier in his sights. The results were devastating: a tumbling AK round would cause immense trauma, and in the heat and mud of the Vietnamese rainforest wounds rapidly succumbed to infection. Morale amongst front-line US troops broke down at an alarming rate. In 1967 a congressional committee of investigation was set up to report on the M16's performance in Vietnam. Investigators found American soldiers who said they 'hated the M16' and picked up enemy AK at any opportunity. (So many GIs threw away their guns in this period that a House of Representatives hearing in 1971 discovered that the US army had attempted to stop the media reporting the habit.) By 1967 US forces were surrounded by Kalashnikovs and America responded to the threat by attacking the supply: from 1967 the Ho Chi Minh Trail was carpet-bombed and the surrounding forest defoliated with Agent Orange. Thousands of Vietnamese men and woman were killed as they attempted to keep the lifeline to the South open, and those who survived had terrible memories of total war being waged from the air against youngsters wearing sandals and carrying AKs.

America would stay in Vietnam until 1973, and the Chinese would supply AKs to the North Vietnamese and to the Viet Cong fighters in the South until 1975, but the AK's moment of triumph came comparatively early in the conflict. In 1968 North Vietnam unleashed the Tet Offensive, a near suicidal ground attack on American forces throughout South Vietnam, and waves of soldiers armed with AKs assaulted US army positions. The resulting TV images of carnage and misery were enough to take anti-war feeling out of the university campuses and into the homes of Middle America. But there was another victor too. When the news showed Viet Cong cadres on the streets of Saigon, attempting to storm the US headquarters in the city, the AK47 reached a kind of revolutionary critical mass on American television. From Tet onwards the AK47 was seen by radical students and intellectuals in the West as the 'anti-imperialist gun', an iconic image of revolution that was more powerful even than the hammer and sickle and still, in the late 1960s, less tarnished.

The bombing of the Ho Chi Minh Trail was four-decade-old history when I met Mr Phan, an official with a Vietnamese delegation to Europe. He was middle-aged with a round belly and greying temples, yet had once been a patriotic teenager with an AK in his hand. Sitting over tea in his office, he took me back to a time when the most powerful nation in the world had determined to crush his own small state. His story, and that of Vietnam, is a key turning point in the history of the Kalashnikov—the moment when the gun became a legend.

Phan was seventeen when he was issued with his Chinese model 56 Kalashnikov at the Revolution Barracks in Hanoi on 3 September 1972. There were hundreds of other recruits being trained at the camp. Some, like Phan, were to go on to be transport troops, but most would join front-line units and go South to fight. There were recruits from all over the North—from Quang Nunh, Hah Tinh and Son La—and people from the same towns and villages naturally wanted to stay together. One group of five girls from Quang Nunh province who had walked to Hanoi to sign up were allowed to stay together, and soon got a reputation for being the most committed cadets in the camp. But generally friends were not kept together and Phan, who was from Cao Bang on the Chinese border, was put into a platoon with a boy called Nong from Hanoi. They were to be trained as truck drivers. Phan had never driven before, but Nong knew how and he helped Phan—in this way the country boy and the city boy quickly became friends. When their driving instructor, Comrade Pho, got angry with Phan for the way he crashed through the gears, forcing the stick through the plate and making the engine scream and burn, Nong showed him how to change gear smoothly and ride the big clutch the Chinese put in their trucks.

As well as their driving course the recruits had to take a basic shooting course. This time it was Nong's turn to struggle, and he failed to hit the targets—the Chinese guns were not very accurate. Phan, who had been taught to shoot in his Communist Party youth group, understood how they worked. These Kalashnikovs were heavy, with wooden butts and a bayonet fitted to the barrel that could be taken off or folded down. The bayonet was three-sided—a long steel triangle—which according to the instructor, Comrade Weh, prevented the wound it made from healing. As he showed them how to stab the bayonet into an enemy soldier and then pull it out again he made a sucking noise. Some of the girls groaned, 'Urgh!', but the instructor said they would be proper soldiers soon and must relish the opportunity to kill the enemy. When the bayonet was fully extended the rifle was as long as some of the recruits were tall.

On the shooting range the first five shots they took were with imaginary bullets. The recruits aimed at the target and pulled the trigger, but in order to save bullets while they were getting used to their weapons there was no magazine in the gun. Comrade Instructor Weh told them that the bullets that missed targets in the practice range could beat the American army twice over. So the recruits would lie down at a distance of 100 metres and aim as if they were going to shoot real bullets. Then, on the command, 'Fire!', they would squeeze the trigger and shout, 'Bang-bang-bang'.

'Any further away and you are wasting bullets again,' said Comrade Weh. 'Maybe you will hit the enemy, but maybe not, and every bullet that does not hit an enemy is a wound in the side of the People's Army and the war of liberation from imperialism.'

Nong did not like pretending to fire bullets and making the noises. 'I feel stupid,' he muttered to Phan, 'helping the war against imperialism by shouting, "Bang-bang-bang". Is this any way for communists to fight? Where is our dignity?'

'Dignity!' shouted Comrade Instructor Weh, who had overheard these remarks. 'Recruit Nong, you are not allowed any dignity yet. You cannot even shoot your gun. Look, all the girls from Quang Nunh province can shoot better than you!'

They were indeed good shots, and when Weh indicated them with a sweep of his hand they all replied at the same time, 'Yes, Comrade Instructor Weh!'

'But you cannot shoot straight, Recruit Nong. If all your wasted "bang-bangs" were bullets, we could pile them this high.' Weh brought his hand up to the crown of Nong's head. 'Enough to invade the USA!' Lying on the ground with their Kalashnikovs, the other recruits laughed.

Like Phan and Nong, the girls from Quang Nunh were to go into the transport division to be truck drivers once they had completed their training. But Comrade Instructor Weh taught everyone who came through his school the same way—he made no allowance for the different assignments that the cadets might be destined for.

'I train you to shoot imperialists,' Phan remembered Weh saying. 'If I had my way I would teach everyone in the country how to shoot imperialists. Shoot well and shoot true! You talk about dignity, Comrade Nong? Learn to shoot straight, and then you will have the greatest dignity—the chance to die for your people. Until then, you shout, "Bang-bang-bang".'

The girls from Quang Nunh laughed, but Nong's face reddened and he looked down. Phan touched his hand against Nong's back. 'It is the same for all of us—we must learn to be good at everything.'

For two days after Weh embarrassed him in front of the other recruits Nong was quiet, and concentrated on looking after his AK. He might not be the best shot in the school—but he would have the cleanest gun. Nong took it to bits three times a day and oiled and rubbed each part. He even oiled the wooden stock, which, very rarely, could dry out and crack or, if it warped, buckle the metal where it joined the stock and make the gun harder to aim.

Phan watched him, but said nothing until the following Sunday morning. 'Come on. I have asked for permission from Weh to do extra shooting practice. Come with me—I will give you a lesson.'

Nong, still stuck in his gloom, shook his head. 'No. I will have a clean gun and a good truck, but I will never be a great shot.'

'Do you think the girls from Quang Nunh province will walk along the road with a man who cannot shoot straight?'

The seriousness on Nong's face slipped a little. 'The girls from Quang Nunh are not interested in walking along the road with boys. They are just interested in defeating imperialism.'

'Perhaps, but when we kick the imperialists out of Vietnam we will have to fill the space they leave behind with more Vietnamese people, won't we? So chasing girls from Quang Nunh province is just as revolutionary as fighting the imperialists and their puppets.'

Nong considered this dialectical observation, then smiled. 'Okay, but just one lesson—and if you can't teach me to shoot straight today, then that's it.'

'And what if the Americans come and you can't shoot?'

'I'll chase them with my truck!'

On the shooting range Phan's voice changed from its soft country tone and became demanding. 'Right, let's start from the beginning, Comrade Recruit Nong.'

'Take it easy,' said Nong. 'You are not Comrade Weh.'

'I must be as serious as he is if I am going to teach you how to shoot. So let's be serious now.'

Both young men stood to attention, then reached across their chests with their right hands to the front of their tunics where a banana-shaped brown cotton pouch hung in which the magazine was carried.

'You know the drill,' said Phan. 'Take out your magazine and tap.' And so, to ensure that the rounds were sitting correctly on the spring and ready to be fed into the firing chamber of the gun, they knocked their magazines against the concrete blocks that had been laid on the dirt floor of the shooting range to mark the firing positions. After that they slotted the magazines into their rifles and then pulled back the cocking handle, which, with a cracking, metallic noise, took the first bullet from the magazine and pushed it into the firing chamber. Both AKs were now loaded.

'Enemy coming, in the woods ahead!' said Phan, dropping down. Nong followed his lead. Both men sank soundlessly to their right knees, their plimsolled right feet sticking out behind them for balance and their left feet pointing forward in the direction of the enemy, each man part of his gun.

'Pick semi-automatic,' whispered Phan. The men reached their left hands over to the right-hand side of the gun, and clicked their fire levers down from the safe setting two clicks to semi-automatic. 'Find your target,' instructed Phan. One hundred and fifty metres ahead of them, in front of an embankment made from bomb-site rubble, were a number of paper cut-out drawings of imperialist soldiers. They were big, bigger than Vietnamese, and bearing down on them with their M16 rifles.

As they aimed, Phan whispered again. 'The AK will always veer a little to the left of the target. If you compensate by aiming a little to the right of the target you will hit often enough to pass the course.'

Phan pressed his AK against his cheek and aligned the front and back sights on the suggestion of a shallow depression at the base of the paper imperialist's throat. This was the vulnerable point, above the flak jacket and below the helmet. Nong did the same. Both men were quiet now and focussed on what they were doing, sweating gently in the morning sun.

'Now squeeze. But gently—the trigger will go back further than you expect before the gun fires.' The two men squeezed and the chat-chat-chat of semi-automatic fire burst across the shooting range. As it did, the throat of Nong's paper soldier disappeared.

Thirty years later the middle-aged diplomat sat in his office and laughed at the memory. 'He wasn't a very good shot at all! But we all had a duty to learn how to kill the invaders.'

Long before, at that moment of triumph on the shooting range, Phan had shouted, 'Nong, you've got it! Why can't you do that with Weh?'

'I don't know,' said Nong, still looking with wonder at the destroyed paper imperialist. 'I did it!'

'Yes, but in real life imperialists don't stand still for us, so we should try some more.'

Nong passed the shooting course.

The driving instructor was Comrade Pho. The recruits would practise their driving in the morning, stop for rice, and then after an hour of physical training in the afternoon they would gather on the parade ground for a lecture by Comrade Pho. 'Our war against America and its puppet in the South can only continue as long as we can supply our troops.' Comrade Pho took a stick and marked out the long, gentle S-shape of Vietnam in the sand of the parade ground. 'Here in the west, where we meet Laos, there are mountains and forests. Through these mountains and forests there is a road.'

All the cadets knew about the Ho Chi Minh Trail was that it was named after their country's leader and had first been used against the French when they were being thrown out of what was then Indo-China in the early 1950s. It was a supply route that bypassed the lowlands where Westerners could fight and took to the dense forest on the shoulders of the mountains.

'Sometimes there are landslides and we lose a road. Sometimes a road just disappears in the jungle,' continued Comrade Pho. 'It is not one road but many, like a river made from different streams. The roads you will drive along will not be like the road we drive along here in Hanoi. Sometimes it will not be there. Sometimes it will be there, but you will not see it at first. But there will always be a road, because the road keeps our struggle alive. If you cannot find a road, make a new one! That is why there is a shovel and a pickaxe on your truck. Why do the Americans bomb the mountains? Because the road is everything. If they can destroy the road then they can destroy our army in the South by denying it food and bullets. So you will be bombed. But I have been bombed and I am still here—the Vietnamese people can overcome any attack by the imperialists.'

'What was it like when the Americans bombed?' asked one of the girls from Quang Nunh.

'It's like the wind, if the wind came from hell,' Comrade Pho answered. 'Or like the sun, if the sun came to earth.' Phan's stomach tightened as he thought of the sun coming to earth. 'It will be terrifying, but it will pass,' continued Comrade Pho. 'We are fighting against a country that thinks it is the strongest in the history of the world, but really they are weak. Our road is stronger than their bombs. Whenever you are scared for yourself or worried about your own life, tell yourself you are not important. On this truck there are enough blankets for two hundred men. Enough rifles for five hundred men. Enough food for a thousand men. Who cares about your lives, comrades? Your truck is everything. Your truck is the life that matters, life for the struggle. If the bombers come you must take your truck the other way, but not too far off the road—a lost truck is the same as a destroyed truck. Take your truck off the road and get out and cover yourself. But before you cover yourself be sure your truck is under a tree— anything that might help it survive. And never hide under your truck unless you have to.'

'Why not, Comrade Pho?' asked Nong.

'A bomb on a truck destroys a truck. A bomb on a truck with a driver hiding under it destroys a truck and a driver. And always get your AK out of the truck! What if you survive but your truck is destroyed? How can you fight without a gun? Put this in your heads and learn it—every time you get out of your truck in the jungle or in the mountains, get your AK first. Before you open the door! Understand?'

After three months at the Revolution Barracks Phan and Nong were given two days' leave. It was not long enough for Phan to go to his parents' house in Cao Bang; it would take him a day to get there and a day to get back if he was lucky. So Nong invited him to come and stay at his parents' house in Hanoi. They dropped their trucks at the depot where two fresh drivers were waiting to take them straight out with more supplies. Phan felt strange about someone else driving his truck but Nong told him it wasn't his truck but the people's truck and, just like a gun, if he put it down he should expect someone else to pick it up. Then the two junior soldiers walked to Nong's parents' house on the west side of the city, near the party headquarters where Nong's father worked as a clerk.

Nong's father was an honoured comrade, one of the five thousand who had joined before the 1945 revolution, and on a shelf at the house stood a photograph of him with a delegation of party members meeting Uncle Ho. Decades later, Phan was still impressed. 'Nong's father had met Ho Chi Minh! That was an incredible thing for me then, to meet someone who had talked to Ho Chi Minh. I asked him what it had been like.'

'He was inspiring,' recalled Nong's father. 'He told us he had no doubt that we would win our struggle because the imperialists' might and their machines were nothing compared to the will of the people. That was when we were fighting the French, but the same is true now we are fighting the Americans.'

'But we have machines now,' said Phan. 'The Russians send us jets and artillery, and the Chinese send us trucks and guns. My truck is Chinese, my AK is Chinese. They are presents from our fraternal comrades.'

'Perhaps, but it is good for the Chinese to see how their AKs work against the Americans. Anyway, if they took your Chinese truck and your Chinese AK47 away you would still fight.'

'Of course!' said Phan.

'Do you think an American would fight without B52s and helicopters?'

On the second evening the two comrades went to a lecture at a cinema in Hanoi. A captain who had been designated a Hero of the People's Armed Forces for fighting in the South had come to talk to them about how a soldier in the People's Army should behave in battle. The lecture was for troops in front-line combat regiments only, not the transport battalions, but Nong's father was able to bring them tickets from the party offices. Over four hundred soldiers forced themselves into a hut intended for half that number, and there was some delay while the crowd got itself settled. When the soldier eventually started speaking it was as if the battlefield had come into the room. He was hushed when he talked of stalking the enemy in the jungle or the endurance required for reconnaissance missions, but when he talked of springing traps and mounting an attack he shouted and opened his arms wide to express the enormity and excitement of the People's Army rushing forward against the imperialists.

'When you go into battle keep quiet and use your senses. Sometimes you will be able to smell the Americans.' The captain brought out a bottle of Old Spice, poured some on to his hand and then flung it out across the room. The soldiers laughed—the smell was strong and sweet. 'You can smell his cigarettes and his chewing gum as well. Keep quiet and you will hear him. The ordinary Americans make a lot of noise, but special troops, the Rangers, the commandos that they drop behind the lines to attack our transport lines and mount ambushes, are different.'

Nong nudged Phan. 'See, they send their best men against us!' A girl in uniform in front turned her head to hush them. It was one of the girls from Quang Nunh. Phan mouthed sorry and smiled, but she did not smile back.

The captain continued. 'They are quiet and they use our weapons.' As he said this he picked up the AK. 'But remember, he can hear you too if you are not careful.'

The audience murmured to itself. Weren't Vietnamese soldiers always quieter than Americans? You could hear American soldiers coming from a great distance. They would shout at each other and crash through the jungle.

The captain hushed them. 'Quiet now, listen. If you are in an ambush, what is your great advantage? Surprise. And surprise depends on two things—not being seen and not being heard. So be quiet, everyone. Completely quiet.' The officer motioned with his arms for them to stop talking until the hubbub subsided. Phan thought the girl was going to shush Nong again, but she looked straight ahead at the officer. She was a very serious comrade.

Once again the officer picked up the AK from the table in front of him. Then he looked into the eyes of the crowd and shouted, 'Lights!' The fluorescent tubes above them flickered and then went out. Everything was dark and quiet.

'An ambush is only successful,' the officer continued, 'if the enemy cannot hear you or see you. I am ready to fire. No one can see where I am. So now I select semi-automatic.' As he shifted the fire selector from safe to semi-automatic in the darkness there was a clack that echoed out across the room. It must have been a prearranged signal, for the soldier at the back of the room immediately turned the lights on again to reveal the instructor looking at his gun. He was bent double, ready to be shot rather than shoot, and seemed to have real fear in his face. It was a startling change. 'So, because I made that noise I gave myself away. I am the hunted now. I am in an ambush.'

The instructor brought himself up straight again and smiled. 'Staying alive is about doing simple things—obvious things, if you stop to think. Comrades, always stop to think, and when you go into combat with your AK be sure to wrap tape around the fire selector lever first.' He put the AK back on the table. 'Otherwise you will be the target for the imperialists.'

The lecture continued for another twenty minutes, but the instructor failed to surpass the dramatic effect he had made with his illustration of the dangers of the fire selector lever. Phan didn't listen carefully to the end of the lecture anyway; he was thinking about combat. He decided that he would tape up his lever that evening so he didn't forget. Afterwards, as he and Nong walked back to Nong's parents' house, he saw the girls from Quang Nunh. Phan left Nong and walked over to the serious girl.

'I know you from the barracks. What is your name?'

'Anh.' Phan waited for her to ask his name but she didn't.

'How did you get here?'

'We were given tickets by Comrade Pho.'

'Where are you staying?'

'We are going back tonight. We brought our truck.'

'Did you enjoy the lecture?'

'Yes, he was a very experienced man. His advice was practical.'

'Not practical for us, though. We won't be setting any ambushes—we are going to drive trucks.'

'Comrade Phan, you cannot say what we are going to do. The war against the imperialists obliges us to do whatever is asked of us, so we must learn to do as much as possible. That way we serve our people best.'

'So,' thought Phan, 'she knows my name.'

After the girls had driven off in their truck, Nong teased Phan. 'She's not interested in you, Phan, just in "the greater cause" and "smashing the dogs of imperialism".'

'You are only saying that because you like her yourself, Comrade Nong.'

As they laughed, the sirens went. A bombing raid was imminent.

'Quick!' said Nong. 'To the shelters.'

All too soon their leave was over and they had to return to barracks. They had learned to drive on the parade ground and then, when they could make the big trucks turn, stop and accelerate on command, they went to the fields outside the city to train in something closer to the conditions they would encounter on the Trail. Although Comrade Pho told them that this was nothing compared to the mountains and jungle, it was the only experience they would get of driving on rough terrain. A week before they were due to complete their course Phan, Nong and five others were driving their trucks back into Hanoi when a flight of twenty B52 bombers appeared above the city. When bombers came, their orders were to go to the nearest shelter. If there were no shelters near by, then there were concrete tubes in the ground into which two men could squeeze if they were frightened enough. But on this occasion Comrade Pho made them stand alongside their trucks with their rifles and addressed them in the midst of the noise and confusion created by the raid. The falling bombs were only two kilometres away.

'Now, did everyone remember to get their rifle when they climbed out of their cabs?'

The cadets shouted, 'Yes, Comrade Pho!', but their eyes were on the bomb blasts that seemed very close now and their ears were deafened by the anti-aircraft unit on the other side of the road that was pumping shells into the sky. Pho followed the young soldiers' gaze, then turned back to them. 'You are safe. Read the direction of the bombs and the planes. They are going away from us. There is no need to run away from your trucks or panic and crash. Use your eyes and you might survive. You are training to drive into war. You are soldiers in the People's Army and you are important—but you are not as important as your trucks or your guns.'

Six months after starting their training Nong and Phan stood on the parade ground of the Revolution Barracks in front of a row of new Chinese trucks. The cabs had wire mesh over the windows to protect the drivers from blast damage, and the back of each truck was ringed with steel hoops over which a brown tarpaulin was draped. Between the men and their new trucks stood Comrades Pho and Weh. Now that he had been given his own truck Phan wondered if he would be able to be brave, to be a good comrade, if the Americans bombed him. They were addressed by a general whom they had never seen at the barracks before, 'Comrade recruits—or, rather, new soldiers of the People's Army!' The men and women on the parade ground cheered at the general's joke. 'Your job is the most important in the war,' the general continued when the laughter had died down. 'Comrades, it is up to you to organize the channel to supply everything for our army.'

They started riding the route in the summer of 1973. The first month they drove down from Nghá An province, where Uncle Ho came from, to the crossing of the Ben Hai River that ran along the 17th parallel. The parallel marked the official border of North Vietnam. South of this line they had to be extra-secretive as they were in breach of international law by transporting arms across it and they were also nearer to the enemy ground forces. Only the best and most experienced drivers worked on the Southern half of the Trail. Phan and Nong would learn their trade on the Northern half and then, when they were experienced enough and had been bombed a few times, they would be sent to work on the other side of the parallel. The men from the South were friendly enough with new recruits; these were the drivers who would take over from them eventually. None of them thought they were better than Nong or Phan just because they had been fighting longer—not even the men who had fought the imperialist commandos in the jungles. The two newcomers would ask the men how things were going in the South. 'Bad,' the men would reply, but that was a good sign because it meant that the Americans and their puppets were scared now and were throwing everything at the route, desperate to stop the supplies getting through. The enemy had even dropped some troops into the jungle to attack them. The Vietnamese had been confused at first, because the Americans had been using AKs.

Still Nong and Phan didn't see any bombing. They took their loads of guns and blankets, rice and bullets to meet the Northbound trucks at the exchange point by the river, and swapped their loads for wounded men and broken equipment to take to the hospitals and repair shops in the North. The two tried to drive close to each other when they could. When the convoy stopped they would cook food together and share a cigarette afterwards. If no bombers came, it took four days to drive down to the river. During the day they slept under the broad green canopy, which was full of sounds that Phan did not recognize. He preferred the day to the night because he could not get used to the noise of the jungle. At night it was either very still and quiet or there was a mad chatter from animals that made him think of the spirits and ghosts that his grandmother had told him lived amongst the creepers and tall trees.

Phan knew he was lucky to be delivering supplies. They didn't starve and they didn't go cold. If it was raining he could shelter, and his truck was full of clothes and food. Apart from a sack of rice they had a bottle of fish sauce and some water. In their cabs they each had a pickaxe, a shovel and a Chinese model 56 AK that hung behind the driver's head. They were told they could bury this gun in mud and it would still shoot. Phan regarded this as ironic. Many of the truck drivers had been buried in mud and most of them were never dug out. If they were, they certainly didn't work as well again.

Hu, the oldest driver in their unit, was nearly thirty and had been driving up and down the Trail for four years. Hu would join Phan and Nong in the morning after breakfast—which was really their evening meal—before they went to sleep, and would talk about the South and the war. One morning he found Nong cleaning his gun.

'You should clean that more often, Nong.'

'But this is an AK, it always works,' replied Nong. 'And anyway, what does it matter if it doesn't work? I don't think I'll ever get the chance to use it against the imperialists. Nothing ever happens up here. I want to go south of the river.'

Hu laughed. 'You will see something happen soon enough. Anyway, you might not have to wait until you go to the South. Why do you think we sleep with our AKs by our side? Because we could meet danger at any turn.'

'What, here?' said Nong disbelievingly. 'Above the river?'

'Yes, of course. The Americans and their stooges have commando squads that they send in to look for the route and ambush us.'

'How can they come this far? Our armies are pushing them back all the time, and the North is so far from their bases.'

'These are special groups—a mixture of US and South Vietnamese soldiers, no more than twelve in a group. They are not boys who are made to come here, and they are not soft and fat like the pilots who come down in parachutes when our rockets hit their planes. They are hard, and you cannot smell them or hear them. They are almost like Vietnamese. They drop into the jungle from helicopters and they look for the road. Their job is to attack the road, then another helicopter comes and collects them if they are successful.'

But for the next month there was no sign of American commandos or bombers and they drove the route during the day as well as at night, getting to the river in under three days. If they saw a deer in the woods they were allowed to shoot at it, but only on the first stretch of the journey. Hunting wasn't good with an AK, which would tear the animal to bits, but Hu had an old rifle from the time of the war against the French and in the second week he killed a deer with one shot that went into its ear. They roasted the animal in the first light as the dawn mist steamed off the jungle, and spent the rest of the day feasting. The smell of the cooking meat attracted other drivers.

'And guess what?' Phan asked me in his office. 'One was Anh.' After the feast, when Phan went to lie down in the woods, he did not go alone.

When the bombing came it was beyond anything that Phan or Nong could have imagined. Phan was thinking about Anh when the raid began. It was three weeks after he had found Anh again, and although they were in separate divisions Phan was happy to know that they were working the same route. Would they perhaps share a convoy? His heart raced a little at the prospect. They were one day's drive from the river, travelling through thick rainforest in a big convoy, a line of one hundred trucks snaking through the forest. Phan was driving behind Nong and they were just pulling off the road to rest for the day. Phan turned off his engine, but when he got out and on to the ground he thought it was still running because the earth was shaking gently. Something strange was happening. Nong looked into Phan's eyes, questioning his friend without speaking. Bombers! Both men jumped back into their cabs, drove their trucks further into the jungle and turned off their engines.

Phan nearly forgot his AK. 'Stay calm,' he said to himself. 'Remember, you are a soldier in the People's Army. You are stronger than the imperialists.' He recalled reaching behind his seat and unhooking his AK. 'Other drivers were coming together. An officer told us, "Don't worry—we are three or four kilometres from the bombs. They will miss us and they will miss the road."' Phan was relieved to hear it but he could hardly believe the bombers were so far away; the ground was shaking much more now and the noise was becoming unbearable.

The officer reappeared. 'We must go further in—return to your trucks.' Above them monkeys were screeching with terror and scrambling through the high foliage and branches. 'Follow the monkeys! Go the way they go!' someone shouted. He did as he was told, and when the jungle got too thick to drive any further he pulled up next to a giant trunk, jumped out and ran further into the undergrowth. All the time the ground was walloping and groaning beneath them. A giant appeared to be striding towards them, his steps coming every three or four seconds, and as he stepped the ground bounced sickeningly up and down. Leaves and branches showered down from the canopy overhead. Terrified, Phan jumped behind a tree and dug himself into the ground with his hands, tearing at the leaves and moss, digging down until he was under the soil, willing the jungle to take him in, to protect him. After fifteen minutes the bombers passed on, and the men gradually came out from the holes and gathered together. The officer reappeared. 'Quick, start your trucks. Let's get back to the road.'

Over the next month Phan and Nong were bombed several times as the enemy planes looked for the road in the jungle. The raids were incredible, as if the imperialists had declared war on the land itself. Did they want to win so much that they would attack the trees and the mountains? Phan started to hate the imperialists in a new way. Previously he had thought of the Americans only as the enemies of the Vietnamese people, but now he realized they were the enemies of the earth.

On one trip to the river the rains were so bad that the road itself became a river, making it impossible for any of the trucks to set off on the next leg of their journeys, North or South. Everyone had pulled up their trucks under the trees, forced to wait until the rain stopped. From there the drivers watched the labour squads, lines of women with AKs and shovels, digging channels to direct the water away from the road. But even these women, who were known as the hardest workers in Vietnam and whose palms felt like the bark of a tree, could not keep the roads open. The rain fell in waves for three days. It washed earth down from the slopes and on to the road. It seeped into every crevice of the men's clothing and broke through the tarpaulins to soak the loads on their trucks. Like two rats from the river, Phan and Nong sat in the damp and shivered until they were invited into the back of a better truck which had a plastic cover rather than a tarpaulin and was still keeping the rain out. Inside were a driver, a soldier and a commissar. They were waiting to go North to the regional headquarters, and they had an American gun they had found. 'It is an M16 but they have just dropped it—thrown it away,' explained the commissar.

'Why would they do that?' Phan asked, turning over the plastic and black carbon composite weapon in his hands. It was much lighter than his AK.

'The Americans are not stupid,' said the commissar. 'They have learned that the AK always works and that it is better at stopping men. An American soldier wears a helmet and special vest to stop bullets, but if an AK bullet hits him here or here,' the commissar touched his shoulder, then the top of his leg, 'the bullet travels through him, and as it travels it turns over and over, slicing his organs into pieces. It goes behind his vest and helmet—it goes behind his armour.'

'The Americans found their men with holes in their legs where the bullets went in,' Phan confirmed to me decades later, 'but when they took their vests off the men would start screaming because underneath their stomachs would be hanging out of their shirts. Men with small entry wounds, little bullet holes, were destroyed. And the wounded men the Americans thought would survive got infections and gangrene, no matter how many antibiotics they gave them. When they found the bodies of our comrades who had been dead for days or even weeks the Americans discovered that their AKs still worked, even if they had been in mud or rained on for day after day. So the Americans gradually abandoned their own gun. They couldn't do it officially—imagine them admitting to the world that a twenty-five-year-old socialist gun was better than their modern capitalist gun—but their soldiers started to use it and their officers let them, even though the imperialist generals said in their newspapers that it wasn't happening.

'At first, whenever the Americans took prisoners or captured an arms dump or one of our forward bases they would give the guns to the tribesmen they armed against us in the jungles in Laos. But eventually they started to keep the AKs for themselves. They had discovered that the AK is the best gun for fighting in the jungle. You know what it is like—you can drop it in the river and it will still work if you are quick enough to get it out. But an M16 stops working if you spit on it!

'So the Rangers came with AKs, and when they opened fire no one shot back at them at first. These were men who had not been down in the South for long and they did not know how things had changed. When they heard AKs they thought the shooting was coming from other soldiers of the People's Army or from the National Liberation Front. Many men were killed, and trucks lost, before they realized that it was not their own side shooting.'

One day the drivers were called to an open-air meeting at the supply regiment base in Hanoi, where they were to be addressed by a senior general in charge of air defence for the central and northern region. The parking area was cleared and swept and a wooden bench placed in the centre. A commissar arrived from party headquarters with a group of officials. Phan and Nong saw Nong's father in the group, but Nong said it would be lacking in dignity to wave. The drivers were lined up on parade with their AKs in front of them and wore pouches full of ammunition magazines—four hung from each driver's chest.

Nong whispered to Phan, 'They cannot expect us to fire all this ammunition from our trucks. It is for our morale, to make us feel braver, to convince us we are soldiers.'

'Perhaps,' said Phan. 'But if we do meet Rangers I will be much braver with four magazines than one.'

The general arrived. He was fat and starting to go grey at the temples. His face was open and his eyes smiled as he went up the row of drivers nodding at each of them, stopping occasionally to talk. When he reached the girls from Quang Nunh province he asked them if they were strong enough to carry so much ammunition and an AK. All five responded as if one person, 'Yes, Comrade Commissar!'

A box was brought out and the general stepped on to it.

'Comrades, this mission is the most important that you will ever go on for your country. The People's Army is about to launch a great attack in the South, an attack that will crush the imperialists and their servants. The supplies you take down the Trail will make that attack possible. Without your success and your bravery it cannot happen.'

He paused to emphasize the gravity of the moment.

'When you supply the forward units of our forces you are like the blood and nerve system in a human body. You must try your utmost to fulfil your task. Comrades, this job is so vital the whole success of our cause depends upon it, but it can be beaten if the enemy finds out what we are doing. You must keep everything secret so we can defeat the enemy. The struggle insists on revolutionary discipline. Do not tell your family what you do, do not tell them when you are going away, where you are going or for how long you are going. Do not tell your sweethearts why you must leave them.'

Phan looked across the circle in front of the commissar as he said 'sweethearts' and into the face of Anh. Either she had not heard the word or was applying revolutionary discipline to her emotions. She did not look back, but raised her chin a little higher into the air and applauded the general.

The Americans found the big delivery. Phan and Nong were in the second half of a column of ninety trucks, but when they were forced from the road the blast was already tearing the leaves from the trees and burning the soil beneath their feet. They stopped their trucks, then ran for a hundred metres before dropping down into one of the clefts in the trunk of a caboa tree to hide. Ahead of them the road turned westward and the front half of the column—thirty-five or forty trucks—had driven straight into the killing zone. This unit had included the trucks driven by Anh and the other girls from Quang Nunh.

When the storm had passed, Phan and Nong emerged from their hideouts. Two hundred metres in front of them the black earth marked the edge of the death zone. The column had been consumed from a point just after the girls' trucks had entered it. Only their last truck remained, smouldering on the edge of the black valley that stretched for five or six kilometres ahead of them. Phan wondered if it was the first of the surviving trucks or the last of the destroyed ones. There was a survivor, but he was sure it was not Anh. She had disappeared, evaporated along with her truck. No one could tell who the survivor was. All the hair on her head and even her eyebrows and eyelashes had been burned off and most of her clothes were gone. Her mouth and tongue were so badly burned that she couldn't speak. She just made a noise, a low animal sound. A soldier next to Phan said, 'She has gone mad, comrade. She lives with the spirits now.'

The bombing had destroyed everything. The earth was smoking, and hissed where napalm was working its way down through cracks in it. The craters left by the bombs were hundreds of metres across, and the earth inside them had reached such a high temperature it had turned white. There was no living vegetation inside the death zone, just some stumps from the larger trees at the edge where the force of the explosions had dissipated. Further inside the zone the surface of the earth had been blasted and burnt away.

The column of men and trucks went back into the woods and started to build a new road under the trees.

Peace talks in Paris continued. Occasionally, comrades went back to base or into Hanoi, where they would be given a talk by a political commissar who would tell them that the Americans were about to surrender and the talks were just a way to allow them to do it without losing face. They knew they were beaten, and they were desperate to leave Vietnam.

Then Phan's column was bombed again. The earth was rising and bucking beneath his feet. He had been thrown out of the cab and he was determined to get back in again. The air filled with the fine mist created by pulverized trees and vaporized mud. Phan was on the very edge of hell. As he struggled to open the door, his sense of colour deserted him and everything he saw became black and white. Through the trunks on the other side of the road he saw Nong waving and shouting for him to come back, but Phan kept going. He pulled the door open and the cab rocked, trying to throw him off before he could get in. Phan kept struggling up until he was in the driver's seat. A stick of napalm must have landed nearby because the world turned first orange, then yellow, and finally a blast of heat forced him to cover his face with his hands and scramble under the dashboard where he watched through his fingers as the plastic seat cover bubbled, popped and softened. He could feel the hair on his eyebrows twist and curl in the heat, and he struggled for breath as the heat sucked the air out of the cab.

Phan was no longer thinking like a soldier of the People's Army; some other power had taken over his actions, and it made him stronger. Usually he would have run away from the heat, but this time he reached up and took his AK off the hook. He reached behind his seat and brought out an ammunition pouch from which he removed one magazine. It caught against the cotton as he pulled at it, and he noticed that the metal case was already uncomfortably hot. He wanted to pull at the magazine, to tear it out of the pouch, but he made himself slow down and pull the mouth of the pouch wide open so that the snag inside was lifted away from the metal. When the magazine pulled out he pushed it into the AK's holding bracket and snapped it home. He pushed the fire select lever down one notch to semi-automatic and then jumped back down from the cab. Above him the air was full of leaves and burning embers. Through the smoke he could see B52s, vapour trails and sticks of bombs coming down from the planes' bellies. The height of the mountains had the effect of bringing the B52s closer to earth. Usually they would be ten thousand metres above, but the bombers above Phan were much lower than that. Even though he had no chance of hitting the giant planes he brought his gun up to his cheek and, standing alone amidst the wind and the fire, started to shoot at the US air force. He was shooting at the men who had declared war upon the earth, the men who had burned the trees, killed four girls from Quang Nunh and sent another mad.

The gun spat into the air. Phan emptied one magazine, then forced in another and kept on shooting until that too was empty. Then he began to feel dizzy; he couldn't get any air into his lungs, and the heat was hurting his eyes. Above him he thought he saw one of the bombers start to give off black smoke. Finally the air raid finished.

As the men came out of the woods to see what was left of the convoy they found Phan standing with his head down. He was breathing heavily and the barrel of his AK was smoking. Everyone was deafened, and at first no one spoke. Phan looked up, but then his eyes closed and he felt himself fall. Nong ran forward towards his friend. 'Phan! Are you okay? What's happened to you?'

The rest of the men gathered round and Nong reached for his friend's AK, cursing as he burnt his fingers on the barrel. At the back of the crowd a driver looked up into the sky. He brought his hand up to shade his eyes and focussed, then started to jump up and down and yell. Still deafened by the bombs, no one could hear him, but gradually he grabbed everyone's attention by waving his arms and pointing up and away to the east. 'Look! Look! One of the imperialist planes has been hit. It's coming down!'

A bomber had detached itself from the formation that had just flattened the mountain, and the first thing Phan heard as his hearing came back was the men shouting, 'Look, look, you've hit one! You've shot down a B52!'

The plane arced away from the rest, dropped on to one wing, righted itself and then manoeuvred into a flat dive. Parachutes appeared below it. Phan looked down at the AK in his hands, and he started to laugh.

At the General Headquarters of Air Defence in Hanoi men and women of the NVA's transport division were standing to attention in front of the same general who had sent them out with exhortations ringing in their ears. The general had had a busy morning. Because of an air raid it had taken him an hour to drive to headquarters, and before that he had had a long and tiring conversation with a colonel in the Ten Lao Air Defence Regiment about why one of his units would not be receiving a recommendation for bringing down a B52 over their area.

'But Comrade General, men from our rocket formation fired a SAM and the plane came down.'

'Sadly, we cannot guarantee that your rocket detachment were the successful soldiers.'

'You cannot?'

'No, Comrade Colonel.'

'But really, Comrade General, you don't believe that an AK47 could bring down a B52? We have heard that crazy story here as well and we laughed—it is just a story.'

'Well, Comrade Colonel, no one is laughing or calling anyone crazy here.' The general had introduced a sterner note into his voice. 'And when you are fighting a great beast like America and its puppet government in the South stories can be very useful. The whole of Hanoi is taken with enthusiasm for Comrade Phan's bravery and resilience. It is a good story, don't you think? One Vietnamese truck driver versus the American air force?'

'But it can't be done, Comrade General. No one can shoot a B52 down with an AK47.'

'And I am not saying that is what happened, Comrade Colonel—only that we cannot be sure that your brave men were successful with their SAM. I am not giving Comrade Phan a medal for shooting down a B52, but for an act of heroism in the face of an overwhelming onslaught by the enemy. After all, Comrade Colonel, I think that is the history of our struggle. It is our story, is it not?'

The general liked the story. He had heard it from a general in the 3rd Army Supply Division who had come up to Hanoi for a staff conference. And the same gossiping clerk in the general's staff who had told Phan about the conversation with the air defence colonel had been present when the general had said, 'You won't believe what they are saying about one of my men! He shot down a B52 with an AK47.' The other officers had laughed as well. But not the general. The Americans were trying to bomb the Vietnamese back to the negotiating table in Paris. There would be many more raids before they had finished, and the general was interested in anything that helped the people defy the rain of death and horror from the skies. He had sent a propaganda unit to interview the man Phan. They had found him quiet and strained; evidently he had lost a girlfriend recently. Well, too bad, everyone had lost someone—the general had lost count of the friends and family he would not see again after nearly forty years of struggle. The propaganda boys had got a quote out of the man, and a picture was all that he needed. Now there were posters all over Hanoi showing Phan looking up to the sky, his AK in his hands, its silhouette starkly black against the white sky, accompanied by the slogan: 'Be like Comrade Phan—resist the imperialists with your every sinew.'

Phan smiled as he remembered the general's exhortation. 'I think he liked me. I didn't look nervous. He told me things would be okay for me. I might have to suffer for a few years—but I was helping the country survive.'

Phan had already appeared to great acclaim at bomb-sites around Hanoi, and now the general had decided to send him round the factories in the North, maybe to China as well, as the face of resisting Vietnam. Phan said, 'What harm if a few stories were blown up out of proportion? Me and my AK were going to get the city through the next round of bombing. Already civilians were volunteering for anti-aircraft duties—if that's what it took to keep morale up during air raids then let them waste bullets. It was worth it to keep the city going. Indomitable city of a thousand AKs! The general said I would be fine after the war—he would see to it. He would get me a place at college, because it was the duty of my generation to make the country after the war.' Then, after talking quietly to Phan that day at headquarters, the exhausted general appeared to fall asleep.

'Comrade General, Comrade General,' urged an orderly, shaking him.

'Oh, yes!' The general looked around and pulled himself up before embarking on his prepared speech. 'For bravery against the enemy, for service to his people, we confirm Comrade Phan as a Hero of the People's Armed Forces. It is your example that leads us all to victory in this, the second resistance war. We are fighting the US aggressors, a brutal and cunning imperialist ringleader, but we are sure to win. We must firmly believe in the party. Don't be impatient, and shun no hardship. We have behind us the whole-hearted assistance of the brotherly socialist countries.' As he said this the general leaned forward, took Phan's AK from his hands and held it high in the air. 'We also have the sympathy and support of people all over the world. The United States invades our country, but the people of the USA themselves support our just cause. For our part we have the determination to win. Always strive to be better, to do some little thing that advances our fight. If every man and woman is vigilant and tries to set an example in his or her behaviour, then we cannot be beaten. Let Comrade Phan and his gun be an example to you all. If we all apply ourselves implacably to defeating the enemy we will win. Everyone has his part to play. Everyone is a gun, firing bullets at the imperialist enemy. We are resolved to defeat the US aggressors. So we will win. The Vietnamese people will not be defeated by imperialism.'

By the time the general had finished his speech he was shouting, and still waving Phan's AK in the air. The battalion commissar cried out, 'Cheers for the general, comrades!' But everyone was cheering wildly already. The general gestured for quiet and motioned to a soldier from his personal guard. 'Comrade Tan has a poem he would like to dedicate to the heroic men and women of the Transport Battalion of the People's Army.' The soldier stepped forward and declaimed:

The enemy brings us to this fight
Our guns are in our hands
Our rice still verdant, our trees still in bud
Spring comes, birds and butterflies still fly.

After the presentation the general approached Phan. 'No one shoots down a B52 with an AK47, Comrade Phan.'

'No, Comrade General.'

'And yet it seems to have happened.'

'Yes, Comrade General.'

Phan spent four months touring the North and China. In China he was taken to an AK factory to see the women who assembled the rifles in lines that seemed to stretch for ever. They did not stop what they were doing, but merely looked up to cheer as Phan and a party official walked by. Everywhere he went he took the famous AK and held it up to the workers, peasants and soldiers who thronged to see the man who had shot down a B52 with an AK47.

The general did not see the end of the war: he was killed in an air raid in Hanoi. Two years later the People's Army was finally victorious and

Phan's truck was taken away. He was instructed to go to a barracks in Saigon that had been used by the army of the puppet regime. He spent two months occupying Saigon and then he was demobbed. He was not allowed to keep his Kalashnikov.

On 5 September 1972, while the Olympic Games were taking place in Munich in what was then West Germany, eight Palestinian Black September guerrillas wearing plimsolls and tracksuit tops and carrying AK47s in bags climbed a wire security fence and then crept through the Olympic village to take the Israeli team hostage. In the initial attack two athletes were gunned down with AKs. Moshe Weinberg died instantly; Joseph Romano, forbidden medical help by his attackers, bled to death. The Black September men, who demanded the release of 250 Palestinian prisoners in Israeli jails in exchange for the remaining nine hostages, were equally doomed.

The Israeli government refused to negotiate and flew in anti-terrorist specialists to advise the police on the best way to bring the siege to a successful conclusion by force. The West Germans opted for deception, telling the Palestinians they would be flown to Egypt. The two helicopters that arrived at the Olympic village to take the attackers and their hostages to nearby Fürstenfeldbruck airfield were flown by men who knew there was an ambush waiting on the tarmac. The ensuing shoot-out was a disaster that left nine Israelis, five Palestinians and one German dead. The next day newspaper pictures showed the Palestinian guerrilla Khalid Jawad lying dead with a hole from a German bullet in his face and his folding stock AK47 dropped by his side.

If Vietnam had paved the way for the Kalashnikov as an icon of liberation, Munich would be the first signpost on the road to its incarnation as the terrorist's gun and that of the Palestinian terrorist in particular. A letter to *Time* magazine caught the prevailing mood: 'For this thing that they have done in Munich the Black September mob are truly the scum of the earth.' In the eyes of the West the Palestinians became a nation of terrorists, a stereotype they did little to change when, in their struggle to overturn the inhuman conditions in which they had found themselves after the establishment of Israel in 1948, they occasionally lost sight of their own humanity. Now, whenever and wherever a Palestinian raised aloft an AK in resistance to Israel—or, as was more often the case, against fellow Arabs in Lebanon or Palestinian refugee camps scattered across the Middle East—it would suggest a cause, however just its origins, that was tinged with murderous intent. Yet before Munich Palestinian resistance to Israel had been an archetypal case of the Kalashnikov serving the cause of liberation; of the weak against the strong, the oppressed against the oppressor. Had the Palestinians, in their desperation, lost interest in the way they were perceived, or had the gun inflicted its own grotesque trajectory on to the conflict?

Twenty-nine years after the disastrous events in Munich, and two weeks after Arab terrorists crashed two passenger jets into the Twin Towers, I met a photographer at the bar of the American Colony Hotel on Nablus Road in Arab East Jerusalem. The bar was a famous gathering place for war reporters, diplomats and visiting politicians, a good place to pick up the gossip that cities on the edge of war thrive on. Under the pink stone arches of the basement bar you could hear what had happened at the Israeli Knesset that day; which groups were about to rebel within the fractious Palestinian liberation movement; which Arab intellectuals were giving up and leaving the city; which were coming back. The American Colony also served the best dry martini in the city, complete with Palestinian olive.

Pierre Bullant was a smiling face at the bar, like me a little out of his depth and looking for a lead that would explain the situation and get him an entry into the chaotic and utterly compelling world of the Palestinian struggle. Over a drink he told me his story. A thirty-three-year-old French fashion photographer, Pierre had spent the last five years travelling the world photographing anorexic models in expensive clothes. In each country he saw the same things: a luxury hotel, a beautiful location and the best restaurant in town. Now Pierre was looking for the things that fashion photography had so far failed to supply: authenticity, action and perhaps, although he didn't care to admit it, romance. He carried several gold credit cards, £4000 worth of camera equipment and a press pass from the Israel Defence Forces (IDF) media office in Jerusalem that allowed him to pass Israeli checkpoints and enter the occupied territories. Over the next seven months, every time I came to Jerusalem I tried to meet up with him for long conversations in the Colony Bar and gradually pieced together his story. At Pierre's request I have changed his name, but his time in Palestine is real enough and his experience of the AK47 mirrors and reveals the Palestinian infatuation with a gun that has been both their saviour and their curse.

The day after we first met, Pierre entered the West Bank and took a taxi out to the Moqataa, the old fort above Ramallah that dated from the time of the British Mandate that had ended in 1948. Now, despite its ruinous state, it served as the official residence of the president of the Palestinian National Authority (PNA), the aging and Parkinson's disease-stricken Yasser Arafat. The taxi passed through a checkpoint, where the guards chatted to the driver for a moment, then through two inner gates. Here the driver stopped to let Pierre out, saying, 'You are okay here, but don't go right up to the president's building.' The driver drove back to the checkpoint to drink tea with the guards and Pierre was left to wander amidst the rubble. Twenty or so Palestinian security men in olive green uniforms milled about, each of them carrying an AKM. They were conspicuously smart: their boots were polished, their tunics were tucked into their trousers, and their guns gleamed from the attentions of oil and polish.

Pierre began to take pictures as he walked towards a third checkpoint.

A soldier approached him, quietly pointing his AK down at Pierre's feet. Pierre kept on shooting and didn't stop until a casually dressed fat man in his late sixties appeared in the viewfinder, smiling and walking towards Pierre until he filled the lens. The man was friendly and polite.

'Hello. Can I ask you what you are doing in Ramallah?'

'I am a photographer.'

'Really. What kind of photographer—press?'

'A fashion photographer, I suppose.'

'What is a fashion photographer doing in a place like Ramallah?' And the fat man opened his arms to take in the vista of ruins and soldiers. 'Are we to be your models?'

They both laughed.

'No, it's not like that,' said Pierre. 'I'm just looking for good pictures. I'm not sure what I will do with them really.'

The fat man, who was losing his hair and wore a small, slightly comic moustache, offered Pierre a cigarette. He declined, and started to shoot again. The fat man didn't move, so Pierre asked, 'What do you do?'

'I work around here.' The man gestured again generally at the piles of rubble and the circle of troops that now surrounded them. 'I make sure everything is okay…You are taking a lot of pictures. Why do you need so many?'

'Maybe I can sell them—I don't really know. Maybe I can tell your story.'

'And which part of our story is this?' The fat man's voice dropped an octave. No longer easy-going, it became demanding now and distinctly less friendly. 'Perhaps you should stop taking pictures for a moment.'

Pierre could hear the engines of an Israeli fighter-bomber high above them.

'Do you have some professional identification I could see?'

All Pierre had was the press photo card from the Israeli military office in Jerusalem, which allowed him to cross Israel Defence Forces lines and enter the Occupied Territories. He decided against getting it out and instead fumbled around in his haversack until he found his passport. He handed it to the fat man, who had ceased to be amusing.

'French?' More soldiers had come over now, all of them casually pointing their AKs at Pierre's lower legs. 'Where were you born?'

'Near Nantes.'

'Have you ever been to Palestine before?'

'No, just Israel.'

'Where?'

'Tel Aviv once, for a photo-shoot.'

'A fashion photo-shoot?'

'Yes.'

'And have you been to Israel this time?'

'Of course—I had to go through Israel to get here. You must land at Tel Aviv. There's no other way for a foreigner to get into the West Bank now.'

'Yes.' The man held out Pierre's passport towards him.

Pierre shifted his weight from foot to foot, not sure whether to grab the document back or not. He was now in the middle of a circle of six soldiers as well as the fat man, and two more soldiers were walking over towards them. How likely was his story? What was a fashion photographer doing in the West Bank? Pierre began to feel a little panic rise in the back of his throat. Although the fat man gave no command, the circle of soldiers gathered closer around him.

The fat man asked, 'How did you get here?'

'I got a taxi.' Over the shoulder of the soldier standing nearest to him Pierre was relieved to see his driver emerging from the checkpoint hut. 'He brought me. That's my driver over there.'

The driver approached and spoke to the fat man. Although Pierre did not speak Arabic he could tell that his driver held the fat man in great regard. The fat man looked at Pierre as he listened, then nodded and spoke to him again.

'So, you are telling the truth. That's fine. I am sorry that I had to bother you. Everything is good.'

'Yes,' said Pierre, not entirely sure how good everything really was.

'Enjoy your time here in Palestine,' said the fat man. 'I hope you get some good photographs while you are here.'

'Thanks.'

'But be careful. Palestine is a dangerous country.' As the fat man spoke the soldiers moved the aim of their AKs away from Pierre's legs.

When he got back to the car Pierre realized he was shaking. He looked down at his shirt and saw a patch of sweat that formed a moist stain from his navel up to his neck.

'Who was he?' Pierre asked the driver.

'He was from the internal security service. He was checking you weren't an Israeli spy.'

'That could have been bad.'

'Yes,' said the driver, smiling, 'very bad. But I think he likes to fuck with you a little.'

'He fucked with me all right.'

'He's an important man,' said the driver.

'Don't you think Palestine needs a few less important men and a few more soldiers these days?'

The driver's smile dimmed a little. 'He is a soldier. He was at Karameh.'

In the last week of March 1968 the editors of *Time* magazine took a brave decision: they gave their front cover over to an illustration of two Arab men. The first was short, wearing a blue serge shirt, military blouson, wrap-around sunglasses and a kuffiyeh, the black-and-white chequered Palestinian scarf. Alongside the man they ran the simple cover line 'Fedayeen leader Arafat'. The artist had added, emerging from a sandstorm behind Arafat, a Palestinian guerrilla holding a Kalashnikov against his chest. He appeared to be stalking an unseen enemy. Above this second figure ran a further cover line: 'The Arab Commando—defiant new force in the Middle East'.

Arafat was the leader of Fatah, the secular and nominally socialist group that provided the bulk of the Palestine Liberation Organization's guerrilla forces. The wry smile on Arafat's face and the purposeful set of the Kalashnikov-toting guerrilla suggested his movement had staked their claim to the front cover by winning a great victory. But the opposite was the case: Fatah had just lost a battle—as the Palestinians had been losing battles for twenty years.

The latest defeat had come in the Jordanian town of Karameh, which, since the recent Israeli capture of the West Bank in the 1967 Six-Day War, had found itself on the front line. Founded in 1952 by Palestinian refugees who had been forced from their homes by the violent creation of the state of Israel in 1948, Karameh, which in Arabic means 'honour', was initially a collection of shacks on the eastern side of the River Jordan. But by 1968 it was a functioning town with industry and, most importantly for the Israelis, a well-established Fatah command structure and base. It was this base that the IDF would attack. In June of the previous year the Israelis had defeated the combined forces of Syria, Egypt and Jordan, and the last of these had lost control not just of the West Bank but also of East Jerusalem. Israel presumed therefore that the Jordanians would stand aside when the IDF crashed across the river.

The Jordanian government and the Palestinians had been expecting the attack on the Fatah base at Karameh since 18 March, when a bomb planted by Fatah men had blown up an Israeli school bus, killing a doctor and wounding seven children. But on this occasion Arafat chose not to follow the classic guerrilla tactic of instructing his men to withdraw to avoid the superior Israeli force. Instead he decided to stay and fight tanks with Kalashnikovs, proclaiming, 'We refuse to retreat.'

On the morning of 21 March over forty Israeli tanks and nearly fifteen thousand troops crossed the River Jordan and smashed into Karameh. The fighting that followed was uncompromising and vicious. The Israelis believed they were routing out terrorists; the Palestinians were fighting for their national pride. In the Palestinian version of events the battle of Karameh is a Calvary of terrible suffering and eventual triumph. When the IDF entered the town every shack, wall and ditch was defended to the death by Arafat's guerrillas. When the Palestinians began to lose ground in the face of the Israeli onslaught they were joined by Jordanian soldiers who could no longer stand by and watch their Arab brothers being killed. Men took on Israeli armour with nothing more than their guns, while others grabbed sticks of dynamite and flung themselves under the tracks of tanks. After twelve hours of this uncompromising resistance the IDF was forced to pull back across the Jordan.

In the Israeli version of events there was no forced withdrawal but merely a successful and planned operation to destroy a centre of terrorist activity, and the only reason Arafat had escaped capture was that he had fled the town the night before the Israeli attack. The IDF had taken casualties because of the involvement of monarchist Jordanian forces that Israel had expected to step aside as it wiped out the socialist Fatah guerrillas.

Whichever version was true, the physical reality of the aftermath of Karameh was the complete destruction of the town and the deaths of at least 150 Fedayeen fighters and 138 Jordanian soldiers. There were also the smouldering remains of a dozen Israeli tanks and armoured vehicles, plus 29 dead and 60 wounded Israeli troops. After two decades of constant defeat this was more than enough to allow the Palestinians to declare Karameh a unique victory.

The Palestinian version of events spread swiftly and the world, previously convinced that Arabs were incapable of defeating the IDF, was astounded. It was inconceivable that Palestinian irregulars armed only with Kalashnikovs and dynamite had inflicted such damage on the supposedly invincible Israeli assault force. The Palestinians had a new image as a people fighting for their country rather than as a refugee problem. After Karameh Arafat said, 'As long as the world saw the Palestinians as no more than a people standing in a queue for UN rations it was not likely to respect them. Now that they carry rifles the situation has changed.' The Palestinian cause was now painted in the appropriately biblical terms of David and Goliath, but instead of a sling shot David would carry a Kalashnikov. However, the new version of the old narrative would have one major difference: David would lose, again and again.

In 2001 the Palestinians were still losing. Their second Intifada (uprising) in a decade was over a year old when Pierre took a room in a house on the north-eastern edge of Ramallah, and from a cry of genuine rage and desperation their resistance was developing into a murderous and embittered struggle. My photographer friend found the action he wanted, but little romance. The uprising was now characterized by a vicious cycle of Palestinian suicide attacks and Israeli raids on the refugee camps and towns where the Intifada was organized. The IDF was taking an increasingly bloody toll. To prevent the Israelis attacking at will various Palestinian groups pledged themselves to resisting every incursion into the camps. If they fought conventionally they faced impossible odds. The IDF had surrounded the population centres of the West Bank with Merkava tanks, while the air space above belonged to their fighter-bombers and Apache helicopters that regularly fired rockets into the streets below. Against this array of twenty-first-century military technology the Palestinians could field AKs and RPGs (rocket-propelled grenades)—the classic Middle Eastern combat combination used in Yemen, Somalia, Iraq and Lebanon. The RPGs forced the enemy out of his vehicle, and the AKs destroyed him once he was exposed. The chopper crews were wary of flying too low over the camps: although the Apaches were armour-plated on their bellies an RPG could take out the rotor blades, and a lucky burst of AK fire could play havoc in the cockpit. The Palestinians' best chance of inflicting casualties on the Israelis was to draw them into the camps, where Israeli technical superiority counted for much less.

The Israeli troops in the personnel carriers behind the tanks were in no hurry to go into Jenin or Ramallah, where they knew they would be vulnerable in the maze of alleys and the advantage would be on the Palestinian side. Like all Israeli soldiers, they feared the alleys and narrow lanes that were a natural killing ground for infantry. When the Palestinians had been destroyed in the camps of Chatila and Sabra outside Beirut in 1982 it had been Israel's allies in the Lebanese Christian militias who had gone in to do the killing with their Kalashnikovs; the Israeli tanks had stayed on the perimeter letting no one out, only the gunmen in. So now the IDF sat outside the camps again, picking off fighters who came out to confront them and assassinating the leadership of armed groups with bombs and rocket attacks. And Pierre waited for his story.

He was sharing the first floor of a villa with a twenty-nine-year-old British woman called Mary, who worked with women's groups in the town. Upstairs were the rooms of Henri and Sylvester, two Belgian freelance cameramen who, when they could get through the Israeli roadblock ten kilometres south, got their filmed reports out via a TV studio in Jerusalem. To reach the villa after the crossing back from Jerusalem they had to drive through Manara Square, Ramallah's central point—a traffic intersection with a roundabout decorated with five giant concrete lions, each representing one of the five main clans of the town—and then head north through the middle-class suburbs before turning right into a cul-de-sac on the side of the hill that faced east towards an Israeli settlement across the valley. At the entrance to the cul-de-sac a teenager chewing pistachio nuts sat on a white plastic garden chair outside the local Fatah office. He was an extremely serious youth, and to emphasize it he placed an AK across his lap. Pierre greeted him solemnly every time he passed. The youth would nod back, but seldom smiled. He spent much of his time looking at the sky waiting for an Israeli missile attack.

In Pierre's second month he moved into the same room as Mary, and the Fatah office was destroyed by a rocket that killed the young guard.

'He probably didn't see the rocket,' Henri told Pierre. 'They come in very quickly—they are inside the target seconds after they are fired. And they are clever—they don't blow the building up, they go in by the window and blow the building out.'

When Pierre got to the office there was no sign of the youth's body, but the plastic chair was still outside alongside his AK. In the wrecked interior of the building he could find only a burnt toilet brush and some papers to indicate that it had ever contained people. Pierre photographed the wreckage and sold the picture to an American agency. In 2001 pictures of burning buildings still sold well.

Pierre took a lot of pictures over the following weeks. As most of the ministries of the PNA government were in Ramallah so were their myriad security services, the various offices of their customs officials, border forces, and representatives of other political parties and religious movements including Hamas. All the men who worked in these places carried AKs; indeed, it was impossible to walk anywhere in the town without seeing one. Mary told Pierre that she wouldn't be surprised to see a dog with an AK in Ramallah. One morning Pierre sat by the lions in Manara Square and counted twenty AKs coming past in a minute; and whenever anything happened, from an Israeli air strike to an argument in the street, a crowd of men holding Kalashnikovs immediately gathered and impromptu slaughter became a possibility. Even traffic jams became armed confrontations. Pierre saw one driver step out of his car, walk to the vehicle behind whose driver had just blown his horn, and empty his AK into the bonnet.

Some journalists found this casual use of weapons more nerve-racking than the threat of Israeli attack, but Pierre was fascinated by the guns, and as winter came to the West Bank he stopped taking pictures of rubble and aimed his camera at the Kalashnikovs instead. At the same time Sylvester and Henri started to take Pierre along when they went out. They drove him across Israel to the Gaza Strip for the funeral of two militiamen who had been blown out of their car by an Israeli rocket. In Gaza City he saw the streets turn into a giant, pulsing procession as thousands of demonstrators packed behind the two open coffins which were passed down erratically over the heads of the crowd. The people wailed and chanted their resistance: 'Palestine, we give our lives, our blood for you!'

Within the crowd were the various political groups, some pushing hysterically against each other, others quieter and holding themselves apart. The Tanzim, Fatah's swaggering new generation of militiamen, walked with an intense purpose as they formed a solid phalanx at the heart of the crowd and cleared their own pathway, marching six abreast and ten rows deep. Ahead of the Tanzim men and immediately behind the coffins were fighters from the Democratic Front for the Liberation of Palestine, dressed in black shirts and baggy black trousers. Around their necks they wore red silk scarves printed with the DFLP logo—an outline of Mandate-era Palestine being pulled back into the Arab fold by an arrow representing the armed insurrection—and over their heads they had pulled red silk hoods with holes over the eyes to enable them to see out. It was their comrades who were in the coffins, and they crowded noisily behind with their AKs held in the air. At the back came forty Hamas fighters, wearing the green scarf of Islam.

Few of the men marching with Fatah, Hamas or the DFLP had been born when the Palestinians had made their bloody stand at Karameh, but they had been told of the great victory against Israel when they were small children. They had played at 'Karameh' in the street with toy guns, and now they consciously represented its legacy as they offered up their Kalashnikovs for the cameras. For the militants the Kalashnikov was the symbol of eternal resistance. AKs in the air, AKs held in fists—Pierre took hundreds of pictures but in essence they were all the same shot: an angry Palestinian with an AK.

Back in the villa in Ramallah two days later, Henri looked ruefully at the shots that lined Pierre's wall. 'I think you're getting obsessed with Kalashnikovs, Pierre. Like they are.'

'But it is all they have,' Pierre replied. 'It gives them dignity.'

'Have you seen any dignity out there recently? What does the Kalashnikov offer them now except empty gestures? They still lose all the time. Their country is still shrinking. They have nothing—just death.'

The New Year brought the truth of Henri's words. Worn down by the bloody to and fro of IDF attacks, Islamic Jihad and Hamas bomb atrocities, Palestinian society fell into despair. Suicide squads blew themselves up in Tel Aviv, Netanya and West Jerusalem. Initially the attacks were carried out by the militant Islamicist factions, but soon the Fatah-affiliated al-Asque Martyrs' Brigade sent bombers to explode in the shopping precincts, nightclubs and falafel bars of Israel.

The bombs led to more reprisal attacks on the towns and camps. Forced to confront their own powerlessness, the Palestinians turned their anger in on themselves. Vengeance was in the air, and an atmosphere of uncertainty and fear descended on the West Bank. Anyone suspected of betraying the cause was dragged out in front of a wall. Gossip, rumour, family feuds and financial disagreement all played their part, and men who had done nothing were shot down. If they were lucky the gunmen gave them a minute to commit their soul to God before firing.

At night, unable to sleep, Pierre would sit up smoking, arranging colour prints on his wall and considering the shape of the AK. The banana lines of the ammunition clips and the almost feminine curves of the wooden hand grips made for a surprisingly organic whole. But the funerals and demonstrations were no longer enough for Pierre: he wanted to be where the AKs were being fired at the Israelis rather than held up in the air.

Getting to the camps could be easy or impossible. The Israelis had no clear or definite policy on journalists: some accredited photographers were let in, and some were stopped. It depended almost entirely on the state of mind of the senior Israeli soldier on the roadblock. And it also depended to an extent on the quality of the Palestinian driver, who had to be able to negotiate an increasing number of road closures. First Jenin, then Tulkarm, Bethlehem and Hebron were cut off by the IDF. With such severely curtailed travel the Palestinians' vegetable crops rotted in the barns and storehouses, the shops pulled down their shutters and families faced an immediate future with no income. And in the alleys the gunmen waited for the IDF, knowing that eventually they must come.

In February Henri and Sylvester were called back to Belgium and bequeathed Pierre their Palestinian fixer, Selim, a sixty-two-year-old chain smoker who always knew which roads were open and which roadblocks could be passed. He regarded it as a point of professional and national pride that he could go anywhere. He would say, 'Yes, yes, we can get to Tulkarm.' If they were stopped he would always have something up his sleeve: 'There is an old road that goes around the hill—a goat road. We will bend around the hill towards Jericho and then we will come round again. Like goats!' Selim knew the factions and he knew the leaders. He could remember as a boy fetching tea and cigarettes for British soldiers during the Mandate. He had driven these roads when they were Jordanian, and when the Israelis took over in 1967 he had continued to drive them. Selim knew roads that no one else knew, roads that could always get Pierre to the fighting.

At five o'clock one morning in January Pierre's mobile rang. 'I think something may be happening in Jenin today.' To reach Jenin Selim drove his old Mercedes away from Ramallah and down towards Jericho in the Jordan valley. Before reaching the lowest town on earth he turned off the highway and on to a track that led north along the escarpment of the Judean hills. They drove for two hours, passing only Bedouin shepherds tending flocks of sheep, before finally turning left and travelling into a valley dotted with the glasshouses of market gardeners.

At the head of the valley stood Jenin, the most lawless town in the West Bank. The Israelis had destroyed the entire PNA infrastructure in Jenin and the Islamicist groups had quickly filled the gap with their own gunmen. What order there was depended on an uneasy truce between different groups and the Tanzim. There were regular firefights between the militias, and almost total unemployment meant the town was full of young men who could hope for nothing more than the small payment they could receive for joining a militia. Unsurprisingly, the atmosphere was heavy with foreboding and fear.

Selim dropped Pierre at a small office behind the taxi station in the centre of the town; here he was bundled into another car and driven at speed for five minutes half on and half off a steep slope that led to the ridge of the escarpment behind Jenin's southern side. At the very top of the ridge were IDF positions that looked over the town and the entire north sector of the West Bank towards the hills of Galilee. But the Israeli position was set back from the edge of the ridge and the troops could not see anything—or anybody—immediately below them. Climbing through the precipitous streets of the camp, it was possible for fighters to get up the hill without the IDF knowing they were there until they opened fire.

Pierre was taken to a small breezeblock and cement house at the foot of the hill where he was introduced to three men in their mid-twenties, Hussan, Hussni and Ali, along with a fourth, slightly older, man called

Jibril. They wore the international uniform of rebellion—jeans, t-shirt and trainers—and had covered their heads: Jibril had tied a scarf around his face, and the others had pulled on black balaclavas. Jibril, clearly the leader of the group, was breathing heavily but calmly—a man preparing to go into battle. The other three were still checking that their magazines were pushed home correctly.

Jibril spoke to Pierre in English. 'So, you want to stay with us? Keep behind us and to one side. If you are right behind us the Israelis will shoot you. If you go in front of us you will get shot by us.'

The men began to stride up the alleys towards the top of the hill. But as they advanced they began to shrink down to avoid the rounds that were starting to ping along the roofs of the alley. Jibril signalled to them to go faster, making them crouch and run at the same time. As Pierre, bent double, struggled to keep up he began to take pictures. The noise and the heat and the sound of his own breathing were closing in on him now, and then he heard the cracking of a Kalashnikov firing on semi-automatic setting. As they worked their way up the sloping alleyways they encountered other groups of men all on their way to the sound of the firing. All of them were carrying AKs, although very few of the guns appeared to be identical. There were AKMs, Chinese 56s, Iraqi and Egyptian copies, Yugoslav versions, Czech versions and even the Galil, the copy the Israelis had developed after Syrian soldiers with AKs held up elite IDF parachute troops during the bloody struggle for the Golan Heights in 1973.

Pierre was intoxicated by the smell of the greased guns, the intensity of the atmosphere, the sound of the men muttering prayers under their breath, the glimpses of women's and children's faces at windows and above all the AK itself. Soon the lane began to level out; they had reached the top part of the camp. Above them now were isolated villas, and beyond that the scrub-covered summit of the hill. At the very edge of the camp twenty-five men had gathered under cover. Many of them were shouting, but Pierre could not make out what was happening—he could not see any Israelis. But Jibril could.

'Look, look! Over there!' Jibril pointed through the bush at the antenna that gave away an Israeli position. 'They have tanks along the top, but they will not come down the hill from here. They have the town ringed, so when they want they will come in from the bottom. This position is where they stop getting out if we are ever attacked down in the camp. They are like a cork in a bottle, and sometimes we have to shake up the bottle—to put some pressure on the cork.' Jibril laughed as he pretended to shake up a bottle, then, looking like a man lifting bar bells, raised his AK over his head and shot off a short burst of automatic fire.

Immediately heavy machine gun fire came back from the IDF position, and the ground and walls around Pierre exploded with fragments of stone and dust. Dropping his camera, he dived for cover. As he lay in the dirt fighting to control his fear he was astonished to see a group of boys, not even teenagers yet, run out from the camp and start shouting and throwing rocks towards the Israelis that Pierre could still not see.

The machine gun fire stopped and Pierre scrambled to retrieve his camera and start taking pictures of the boys. The nose of an Israeli armoured personnel carrier burst through the bushes a hundred metres ahead of them and automatic fire splattered the sandy soil in front of the children, who ran back into the camp. Then Jibril stood up and started to fire from the waist. Pierre tried to take pictures, but the intensity of fire and noise froze him back behind the wall. Forcing himself to look over the wall again, Pierre could not believe what he was seeing. It was madness. Just as he presumed the man must be hit, Jibril leapt back behind the wall.

'That is enough,' he panted. 'The battle is over.'

On the drive back to Ramallah Pierre nursed his camera and Selim asked him if he had got what he wanted.

'I think so.' Pierre had tasted the war in the camps.

Several weeks later, on a sharp and windy February morning, Mary went out to buy fresh vegetables. As she walked back to the villa, surrounded by others going home to make lunches of fresh pita and salad, she had a sudden and unnerving sensation of time freezing. Everyone around her had stopped and was looking up, apparently bewitched by an apparition in the sky. Mary followed the crowd's gaze to two black spots which hovered and dipped above the town. The wind blew some dust into her eyes and she looked down in order to wipe them with a tissue. When she looked up again the two black dots had come closer and she recognized the wasp-like shapes as Apache helicopters. The spell broke; women started to scream and shouted for their children to come in from the street. Armed men appeared from nowhere and gestured at the sky. The helicopters continued to hover, unperturbed by the chaos and panic below.

Although she was petrified, Mary's feet seemed fixed to the ground. Everyone else was either seeking cover or barking orders, and only she stayed still and silent. She saw the Apaches come together over the northern part of town and realized what was going to happen just as it happened. The two helicopters released a rocket each. Mary instinctively followed the trajectory as she looked across Ramallah to a house on a ridge on the east side of town, and saw both rockets enter the same ground-floor window. There were two loud clumps, and the windows momentarily flashed with a bright and searing orange before the glass burst out. For a few seconds black smoke poured from the shattered windows and broken roof, then a backdraught sucked the smoke back in and seemed to take the noise with it. Within three minutes Kalashnikov-carrying officials from different militias and branches of security had closed in on the burning house. A chaos of wailing and shouting followed, and people began to shoot their AKs into the sky. A man came out of the wreckage holding a human arm.

Mary was crying when she got back to the villa. Pierre was arranging photographs, putting Kalashnikov against Kalashnikov, when she came into the room. She fell on to a chair and sobbed, 'It's chaos—they are being attacked, and they run around shooting in the air. They are like children.' Pierre made her some sweet black tea and lit a cigarette for her, and Mary gradually became calmer.

'It's not the death and the misery, it's the chaos. Why do they just stand there with guns, shouting? What will that do? If they had some sense of order maybe they could do something. What was the point of firing their guns into the air after the helicopters had gone? All this running round with AKs—they are like children,' she repeated.

'They do it to bring the people out,' said Pierre.

'But it's crazy,' Mary replied. 'It makes it worse. The streets were blocked, and they couldn't get the ambulance to the house.'

'It's part of their resistance. They are being defiant. They are saying, "You can never beat us. Our rage is stronger than your rockets and guns."'

'But they're wrong.'

'To us, maybe, but they don't expect to win this war any more. It's not even a war to them—it's just how they live, with a Kalashnikov in their hands. I don't think they can imagine this ever ending now. Why should it? Every year they lose a bit more, every year they are punished for existing. All they can do is try and effect the way they lose. Never stop being angry. That's what being Palestinian means now.'

'So they waste bullets shooting in the air and their streets descend into chaos. How does that help them? That helps the Israelis.'

'It looks crazy, waving guns at a bomb-site. But the guns are all they have got that say they are not completely beaten—that they are men and that the Palestinians are a people.'

'I think they're fucked,' said Mary. 'They are so confused here they might as well start shooting each other.'

Pierre nodded. 'I don't think you can live in this shit all your life without it getting into your head.'

Henri, who had been silently watching, said, 'Perhaps.'

After the rocket attack Mary needed to get out of Ramallah. Pierre took her to Tel Aviv for a week to take Ecstasy in the clubs that he had visited when he was a fashion photographer. They stayed at a luxury beachside hotel whose manager remembered Pierre and gave them the best suite. 'We are', he admitted, looking around the empty foyer, 'not fully booked at the moment.' The couple spent four days taking Ecstasy, watching the sun go down over the Mediterranean, then dancing for hours on the shore and sleeping all morning. But, like the drugs, the pleasure soon wore off for Pierre. As he lay in the sand, feeling the warmth of the winter sun spreading up his back, he took photographs inside his head. Photographs of the Tanzim and Kalashnikovs. Photographs of Jibril. On the fifth day he left Mary in the suite and went back to Ramallah.

Before Pierre could cross back into the West Bank he had to visit Jerusalem and renew his Israeli military press accreditation. The middle-aged woman who dealt with his application in the IDF press office on Hillel Street in central Jerusalem had the sour demeanour that went with the job of presenting the occupation of the West Bank and Gaza as a necessary law enforcement operation. There were four other journalists in the room, all waiting to have their cards renewed. This process could be a formality or she could make it difficult for journalists she perceived to be pro-Palestinian. In 2002 a lot of journalists could be perceived as pro-Palestinian, and that must have included the four ahead of Pierre because he had to wait an hour and a half before he was ushered into the office.

Before her the woman had a number of press cuttings and photocopies of newspapers and websites. From his side of the desk he could see Jibril's arms and his AK in a shot he had sold to a French news magazine.

'You should watch the company you keep. You seem to get very close to the terrorists,' she said.

'I work hard to get my pictures.'

'What about some pictures of our side?'

'There's a picture of them there.' Pierre pointed to a picture of a Merkava he had caught reversing through a garden wall. Exhaust fumes were pouring from its rear as the driver over-gunned the engine in his haste to get out of an isolated position.

'No, I mean taking pictures from our side, so the world can see what happens to our boys.'

'It's difficult. Your boys keep shooting at me.'

'Well, you should be careful.' She smiled for the first time and printed his pass.

Pierre went straight to Jenin to find Jibril and asked him to pose for a series of portraits with his gun. Jibril thought it unseemly for a fighter to be posing for the camera, so he refused to stand still for Pierre. But the other men were younger and less stern and liked the attention. Gradually Jibril allowed himself to be photographed away from the actual fighting, but always with his face covered. A leader was a target who might be betrayed to the Israelis by an informer at any time, and it was imperative that the enemy did not have a good likeness of his face. If Pierre was too good at his job he might get Jibril killed.

This amused Pierre. 'But you make yourself a target every time you fight the Israelis. You stand in front of them and wave your AK. How could you be more of a target than that?'

To which Jibril replied, 'That isn't me—it is a Palestinian fighter. They do not know it is Jibril. They do not know where that fighter lives or the name of his sisters, his aunts, his mother and his father or his cousins. They do not know which houses to demolish. Please, Pierre, do not photograph my face.' So Jibril kept his face hidden with a kerchief while Pierre kept taking photographs.

Pierre took to staying the night in Jenin, sleeping on a mattress on the floor. He sat up late and argued with Jibril, who would defend the Palestinians' right to resist: 'Yes, there is terror and brutality committed in our names. But who speaks of our ruin, our loss, our humiliation?' Jibril spoke with a quiet and intense anger, and didn't shout or rave. He didn't need to—every pore of his skin, every inch of his being attested to his anger. Any number of treaties could be signed with the state of Israel, but Jibril and the men like him could never be stood down; for them, the war could never end. Jibril was the expression of the Palestinian struggle in all its nobility and obsessed hopelessness.

Pierre had developed his own obsession. When visitors came to the villa Pierre would show them his work. A friend of Mary's, a British journalist on his way to Tulkarm—a town that was in the hands of Hamas and had sent many suicide bombers across the border into Israel—looked at the pictures on the wall while Pierre made some tea.

'Your pictures are all of the same thing.'

'What's that?'

'Every shot is about the AK, not the man. Why is that?'

'With these people the AK *is* the man. Look, each one is slightly different.' Pierre moved along the pictures, pointing out the differences. 'This one was outside Jenin. This is a fighter—he has a wooden stock. But this guy was taken in Ramallah. You see, he has sawn the stock off his gun completely so he can hide it in the side pocket of his car door and pull it out from his jacket pocket quickly. He's not a soldier, he's something else—special security.'

The journalist nodded. 'I didn't know an AK could mean so much.'

'AKs mean everything here,' said Pierre.

The fighting around the camps intensified, and Pierre began to take risks to get the shots he wanted. Several times he came near to being hit, and in one firefight a Tanzim fighter shot the heel off Pierre's left boot.

Jibril laughed for half an hour: 'You're a war hero now!'

After this the fighters began to think of Pierre as one of their own, so they were surprised when he stayed away for a week after Hussni was killed. Pierre was alongside Jibril when it happened. A heavy machine gun round went through Hussni's stomach and came out of the back of his neck, taking much of the young man's insides with it. On the drive back to Ramallah Pierre began to cry.

Selim stopped the car in the Jordan valley, went to the boot and retrieved a plastic bag full of figs and a bottle of water. He motioned to Pierre to join him in the shade at the side of the road. When they had sat down Selim began to speak. 'Look over there, across the valley.' Pierre looked out over the scrub and sand towards the Jordanian hills on the other side. 'There is a bridge down there on the river. It's named after Allenby, the British general who conquered Palestine in 1917. When Allenby had chased the Turks out, the British invited the Jews in. The grandchildren of those Jews used the Allenby Bridge to cross the Jordan and attack Karameh.' Selim looked out over the dry valley. 'So that is where we had our great battle, where we began to stop the process that Allenby had started. But we were expelled from Jordan. Not by the Israelis but by Jordanian troops. King Hussein sent his army to kill Palestinian fighters and drove them into Lebanon in September 1971. You know that is how the Black September group got their name.'

Pierre nodded. He knew all the history but he had never heard Selim—lucky Selim who usually laughed at everything, even the helicopter attacks—speak of it before.

As the sun went down on the valley Selim's face fell into shadows. 'And what did Black September do with their Kalashnikovs?' he asked.

'They murdered Israeli athletes at Munich.'

'Yes, and when they were shot down at Fürstenfeldbruck by the German police one of them had left a note on his body, a last will and testament. It said, "Palestinian people. Do not abandon your guns", and we didn't. We went to Lebanon and to another war. And in 1982 the Israelis invaded and beat us again, and they took the captured Kalashnikovs and put them on display in a public park near Tel Aviv, with ice cream stalls and floodlights so families could walk amongst the guns and be sure that the Palestinian terrorists had finally been beaten. And after the exhibition in the park the Israelis gave the Kalashnikovs to the CIA, and the CIA sent them in container ships to Pakistan. In Pakistan they were put in boxes and strapped to mules, and then the Pakistanis drove them over the mountains to Afghanistan to the Mujahadeen to fight the Russians. The first Kalashnikov that bin Laden held was a Palestinian gun given to him by the Americans and supplied by the Israelis.'

Back in the villa Pierre laid his trousers out on the floor. They were marked with Hussni's blood, which had turned from scarlet to a darker red, almost black where it was thickest. There were other stains too, yellows and pinks that were more terrible than blood.

A few weeks later Pierre called Selim in the early hours of the morning.

Selim proved hard to stir, and he was bad-tempered when he finally came to the phone. 'You'll wake my grandchildren, Pierre. What do you want at this time of night?'

'I want to go to Jenin.'

'Nothing is happening in Jenin today. I would have heard something.'

'Look, Selim, I want to be there.'

'Well, you'll have to wait an hour. I'm not breaking the curfew and I must eat first.'

Selim was quiet on the drive, although he dropped his insistence that nothing was going to happen when they found that Jenin had been blocked off. Even at 7 a.m., at a checkpoint five kilometres from the town there was a long queue of people trying to get through to sell their vegetables. Selim and Pierre walked a hundred metres to the head of the queue where a young Israeli officer was holding back a crowd of angry farmers.

'What's happening?' Pierre asked.

'No one gets through today,' replied the soldier sharply. 'What's it to you? You're not getting through.'

Selim stepped forward, smiling, with his palms apart. 'Sir, we're going to see my family. Please, can we get through?'

Anger and fear played on the soldier's young face. 'I thought I told you: no one gets through.'

'Okay,' said Selim. 'Thank you, officer. Good morning.' He turned to Pierre. 'Come on, we'll go home. Today is not a good day.'

But Pierre stood where he was and looked into the officer's eye. 'And what about all these people? What will they do with their vegetables?'

'What's it to you? You're not getting through.'

'They'll starve.'

Other Israeli soldiers, all of them young and wearing sunglasses, began to wander over.

'Don't make trouble here,' the officer snarled at Pierre. 'I will arrest you. You can sit in the back of our vehicle for eight hours if you want. I don't care who you work for. What are you doing in my country?'

'*Your* country?'

Selim grabbed Pierre by the arms. 'Come on, come on,' he urged.

They went back to the car, and Selim drove for five minutes until they had turned a curve at the bottom of the hill and were out of sight of the checkpoint. Then he pulled the car off the road and made a call, speaking rapidly in Arabic for five minutes. Then he started the Mercedes and pulled away.

'There is a way, but it is dangerous. Do you want to do it?'

'Of course.'

They drove east for twenty minutes before turning south at a dead olive tree and on to a dirt track. Another twenty minutes brought them over a small rise and alongside a group of dilapidated tomato hothouses, the plastic sheeting that had once covered them ripped and falling away from the steel frames. Selim walked Pierre to the back of them where an ancient minibus was parked with its motor running.

The driver, young and clearly wearing a pistol under his belt, urged Pierre on. 'Yalla, yalla!'

Pierre jumped in and immediately fell over a plastic basket full of oranges. Four Palestinian women in traditional dress who were packed into the back of the van laughed at him.

Selim slammed his palm on the window: 'Be careful.'

The driver took a winding back route through the scrubby, untended fields towards Jenin. Above them they could see an Apache circling, and Pierre gripped the seat in front with fear. The women, still amused at his fall, chatted on unperturbed, but the driver wound down his window and looked up as he navigated the rutted track that threatened to destroy the vehicle's suspension.

After a quarter of an hour of tense and bumpy driving the van pulled into the centre of Jenin to find chaos. Ambulances were screeching through the streets, women were running to get home with food from the few shops that were open, and from the hillside refugee camp came the steady cracking of gunfire. Pierre ducked into the warren of alleyways and began to run up the hill. He was close to the summit when the sound of rifle fire was broken by a ground-shaking boom and the walls of the alley shook with the percussion. Pierre fell to the ground and rolled into a corner; he had never come under heavy shellfire before, and he struggled to get back the breath that the shock waves had sucked from his chest. After several minutes gasping in the dust he pulled himself together and continued up the alley.

At the top of the hill he found a scene of madness. A crowd of Palestinians were screaming at each other out in the open and at the same time attempting to haul a blanket into shelter. Two hundred metres beyond these figures the giant bulk of a Merkava had smashed through the trees and knocked over some outbuildings; its gun was now traversing the edge of the camp. On the ground a pool of blood was already turning the soil into red mud. A fighter stooped to pick up a Kalashnikov that was smeared with the same blood. Pierre recognized it immediately: it was a Chinese 56 with a dark wooden butt, which he had photographed in the hands of its owner many times. The men carrying the blanket broke away from the crowd and made for the alley. Pierre instinctively brought his camera up to his eye, then pushed it down again as the men came level with him. Inside the blanket were the remains of Jibril.

Later, after Pierre had photographed the fighters running back into the centre of the camp, and been knocked over by another shot from the tank that had left him half-deafened, he found himself in the room where he had first met Jibril. Hussan was lying in the corner, his arm bandaged and his face speckled with sweat. A doctor had been sent for, but none came, and Pierre spent the night alongside Hussan, who moaned in his sleep.

The next day there was a martyrs' funeral in Jenin. The entire town came out, but there was little to bury. Jibril had been caught directly by the shell. The impact had virtually destroyed him and all that remained were his head and a small patch of bloody, tattered jeans below his knees. But by arranging the blanket carefully in the coffin to stand in for his missing body his comrades had created the illusion of a man.

There were six coffins in all, one of which carried the body of a boy who had been caught in the crossfire. Hundreds of hysterical mourners packed Jenin's main street, following the coffins to the burial ground and holding Kalashnikovs in the air. Amongst them were children with

Kalashnikovs of cardboard and scrap wood that had been painted black. Some were as young as seven, but they marched just as proudly as the men. This was the next generation, ready to live the legend that had been created at Karameh.

Two days later Pierre caught an Air France flight to Paris. As he took off, Henri and Sylvester returned to the villa. The house had no shutters and it had filled with dust blown across the road when the Fatah office was destroyed. Pierre had taken only his clothes and cameras; the walls were still covered with his pictures. Henri sat down in the half-light and looked at the pictures. He put his cigarette out on the floor, shook his head and said to Sylvester, 'Too many guns.'

On the morning of March 29 the unmistakable rumble of tanks woke them at seven. Rushing to the window, they were in time to see a line of Merkavas pass the top of the street heading up the slope towards the Moqataa. Three hundred metres above them four Apache helicopters were firing rockets down into the town. The two men rushed to get their camera equipment and two bluebody armour vests on which they had lettered 'PRESS' with black marker pen. Fumbling to put on their helmets they rushed out into the street, which had already emptied of civilians. They ran past the ruins of the Fatah office and down towards Manara Square, where the sound of heavy fighting echoed amongst the statues of the lions of the Ramallah clans. Two IDF tanks had parked in the middle of the square. At its southern entrance lay the corpses of two Palestinian fighters. Above them was a poster of Arafat which an Israeli had braved the hail of AK fire to rip—but then had clearly thought better of it, leaving the president's face clinging half on and half off the wall. A Palestinian Red Crescent ambulance screamed down the road, only to pull up at the junction where the tanks barred its way.

Gunmen lurked in doorways and at windows, disappearing when the tank's cannons traversed towards the direction of the firing. The two Belgians picked their way carefully through the streets, passing more corpses as they got closer to the Moqataa. They came across a tank ramming down a shop front; on the roof above the shop a Palestinian fighter was firing his AK directly down on to the top of the tank. On the other side of the street at ground level, beside the Belgians, a second fighter had taken cover in a doorway. In a desperate attempt to stop the tank he fired an RPG into its tracks. But the track stayed on and the tank pulled back from the shop, bringing down the front of the building and the gunman. The tank then turned its main cannon towards the RPG, and Henri and Sylvester started to run desperately for the corner of the street. The blast blew them off their feet, but despite the shower of shrapnel and stones that flew past them they were uninjured. The fighter with the RPG, however, had been burned flat against the doorway. By late afternoon the Moqataa was surrounded.

It was a week before the tanks pulled out. When they had gone President Yasser Arafat stepped shakily out of the Moqataa, surrounded by his ministers and senior officers. The men around him were in their sixties and seventies; most of them had been exiled with Arafat in Jordan, Lebanon and then Tunisia. Many of them had been at Karameh in that far-off spring when they had seen off the Israeli army. Arafat's hands were shaking. His lips were drawn tight over his jaw and his eyes were sinking into their sockets. The man who had personified the Palestinian struggle was on the edge of giving up the struggle himself. 'We will fight on,' declared Arafat before his guards helped him back into the Moqataa.

On April 5 the IDF invaded Jenin. After four days of fighting the camp was levelled to the ground. Nothing remained of the alleys that fate had made Jibril's home and his battleground. Forty gunmen died in the battle; hundreds more managed to escape with their Kalashnikovs.

By the late 1970s the actions of Palestinian militant groups had dented the AK47's previously pristine revolutionary image. It was now the international symbol not just of justifiable revolt but also of unjustifiable terror.

In the 1980s a phenomenon arose that warped the AK's image even further: the child soldier. Although children with AK47s can be found in Latin America, and amongst the Keren people of Burma nine-year-olds have commanded their own guerrilla groups, it is in Africa that the largest number of underage fighters have been deployed, and that continent has become a byword for the use of children as combatants. Given the millions of AK47s between Egypt and South Africa, those children invariably had Mikhail Kalashnikov's gun in their hands when they went into battle. Yet despite the reports of ten- and eleven-year-olds slaughtering civilians in the myriad of vicious conflicts that dotted the continent from the anti-colonial wars of the 1960s and 1970s onwards, the AK47's grip on the imaginations of artists and musicians in the West would become even firmer.

Africa has become a paradigm of the Kalashnikov society, a land where the sheer numbers of the gun make it impossible for civil society to assert itself and halt the killing. Simultaneously it has become a cultural lodestar in the West, a convenient badge of compassion to be worn by millionaire rock stars with albums to promote. In Africa the Kalashnikov is both killer and advertising executive, and the child soldier has been at the heart of its campaign in both senses of the word. This symbiotic relationship reached its apogee in 2005 when Bob Geldof organized Live 8, a concert for Africa in London's Hyde Park to be broadcast worldwide to an audience of millions. The concert was noteworthy for the almost complete absence of Africans on the stage. The images of suffering Africa—the starving women, the child soldiers—were welcome but the uncomfortable reality was not.

One of the musicians to whom Geldof refused a Hyde Park platform was a twenty-three-year-old Sudanese rapper, a man whose music offers a more authentic picture of Africa under the rule of the AK47 than the work of any Western rock star. Emmanuel Jal was seven years old when the crackle of Kalashnikovs and the thrum of helicopter rotor blades brought war to his village. Late on a warm May morning in 1986 government helicopters swept in from the hills above Tal in the Upper Nile region of southern Sudan to attack the small community of a few hundred people with heavy machine gun fire, rockets and bombs.

The villagers they attacked were Nuer, a tall, black-skinned people who had been fighting Arab invaders from the north of the country for as long as they could remember. The Arabs had first come south two hundred years before as slave traders; more recently they had been soldiers fighting on behalf of the government in Khartoum in a civil war that had been consuming Sudan since it gained independence from Britain in 1956. The conflict had been encouraged, funded and supplied with weapons by the opposing sides in the Cold War, and as a result there were millions of Kalashnikovs in Sudan.

Apart from a decade of relative peace between 1972 and 1982 the village had been at war since long before Emmanuel had been born, since before even his parents had been born. In that time the Khartoum government had been called by different names, but it had always represented the Arab north and it had always been seeking the same thing: the oil beneath the ground on which the Nuer lived.

Emmanuel spent the morning of his last day in his village at his aunt's house. His father had been away for over a year with the Sudanese People's Liberation Army (SPLA), the guerrilla movement that defended the black south from the Arab north. Emmanuel's mother had died when he was five, killed by one of the many diseases that thrive in Africa's conflict zones. Emmanuel didn't know which disease—just, as he was told, that 'the war took her'.

Emmanuel didn't go to school; there were no Christian Aid workers near by, no United Nations camp within eighty kilometres to give children reading books or pencils, and no one in the village to take lessons as all the teachers had joined the SPLA. So Emmanuel had spent this morning like most others, sitting in the doorway of the small single-storey house and listening to the sounds of the village—the whine of overworked car engines, the shouts of the old men and the anguished lowing of a cow on its way to slaughter. As Emmanuel listened he sang quietly to himself and dreamed about going to one of the schools that he had been told were run by Western charities that operated in the region.

Earlier that morning Emmanuel had watched as the women walked noisily down the hill to the market in the centre of the village. As usual there wasn't much food to be had there and later he had watched them walk back again, quiet and disappointed. The little boy had squinted into the bright glare when the sun came over the top of the houses on the far side of the street where the older men sat on the steps and talked as the day edged towards its fiercest heat. Emmanuel knew that the women always went to market and that the men always sat on the steps opposite his aunt's house, but today as he watched he felt something had changed. There was something different in the village air, something he could not explain to himself.

As the sun baked the street four men walked up it from the direction of the market, stirring up the dust as they came. They wore the makeshift uniforms of the SPLA—sandals plus a pair of ancient jeans with a khaki shirt, or threadbare combat trousers and a t-shirt that was coming apart at the seams—and they carried the wooden-stocked AKs that gave them authority in the village. They didn't speak but peered into the shade between the houses and turned their heads slowly, carefully taking in everything around them. Emmanuel realized that the guerrillas too had noticed that there was something different about the village today. He drew in his legs as they approached—he had seen guerrillas kick the village boys who laughed at them and followed them shouting down the street. Even though he could not remember what his father looked like, he looked for him now as the four guerrillas walked by; but, as on every other occasion he had watched SPLA men, his father was not there.

There were no more than twenty guerrillas in the centre of the village that morning—not enough to make the village a valuable military target for the government. But by 1986 numbers no longer mattered in Sudan. Emmanuel didn't know it yet, but the conflict had reached a new stage: no longer a logical if ferocious struggle for resources, it now teetered on the edge of being a war of racial annihilation and national self-destruction. The government was determined to terrorize the Nuer into leaving their homeland. It had bombed schools, burned down houses and sent Russian tanks against SPLA towns and camps. Sometimes the guerrillas were pushed right back into the extreme south of the country, or to their bases across the border in Ethiopia, where Mengistu Haile Mariam's Marxist regime was happy to supply Kalashnikovs and support to anyone who fought its regional rival. They had also been pushed across the Uganda border, where whole armies could disappear. But they had always kept a foothold in their homeland.

Sometimes the SPLA came down from the highlands to capture government positions and hold them for a few days before Antonov transport planes re-equipped as bombers forced them out again by dropping oil barrels full of dynamite and shards of steel. Occasionally the SPLA fought amongst itself when maverick leaders made separate truces with the government to gain temporary advantage in the constant power play of southern Sudanese politics. But always, whatever the balance of power and influence in the region, people died—either in a blaze of Kalashnikov fire or of the disease and starvation that invariably followed the guns.

Sudan was not unique; this was the situation across East Africa and beyond. The land had been in the grip of the Kalashnikov since the old anti-colonial struggles had morphed into Cold War by proxy, and AKs had flooded into the continent from the mid-sixties onwards. The USSR, Communist China and North Korea had sent millions of Kalashnikovs to black Africa; the Chinese and North Koreans had even set up an AK ammunition plant in Uganda. At first these Kalashnikovs had been a symbol of liberation; in Mozambique and Angola guerrillas called their sons Kalash to celebrate the gun's vital role in the fight against Portuguese colonial rule. In 1975, when the Mozambique Frelimo liberation movement finally achieved independence from Portugal, it unveiled a new national flag which featured a ploughshare, a book and a Kalashnikov.

It would be the Kalashnikov rather than the ploughshare or the book that would be triumphant. The continent was buried under millions of small arms and, rather than providing the firepower to win the anti-colonial struggles and bring liberation, plenty and peace, they provided the conditions for permanent conflict in Africa. In Mozambique there would be a further million deaths in the post-independence civil war between Frelimo and the South African-backed Renamo movement, and when that conflict ended in 1992 there were over 7 million automatic weapons in unofficial circulation in the country.

This mad excess of assault rifles affected every relationship. Demobbed government soldiers and rebels, bank robbers, poachers, truculent teenagers and pickpockets all had access to Kalashnikovs, a situation which guaranteed that life could never be normal because there was always the possibility of a burst of automatic fire. Since everyone had one, everyone *had* to have one—Africa existed in a state of Kalashnikov paranoia. For millions the Kalashnikovs brought blood-letting rather than liberty, and by the 1990s 'Kalash!' was a cry of despair rather than of pride. In February 1991, the *Bulletin of the Atomic Scientists* published a list of countries where 'young men (and some women) equipped solely or primarily with AK-47s and other "light" weapons have produced tens of thousands—and sometimes hundreds of thousands—of fatalities...most of the casualties in these conflicts are non-combatants.' Of the seventeen countries the *Bulletin* listed ten were in Africa: Algeria, Angola, Burundi, Congo, Mozambique, Rwanda, Sierra Leone, Somalia, Sudan and Uganda.

In Sudan, war had become the natural state of things. The signs of it were all around young Emmanuel: there was rarely enough food to eat, and most of the men in the village were old. The young men from the village who went away seldom came back. If they did, they had often lost a leg or an arm. But although he knew there were people called Arabs who wanted to kill him, so far the war hadn't touched Emmanuel directly. Until today he had never been shot at or bombed.

When the throb of the helicopters first distinguished itself from the other sounds that filled the village Emmanuel was still sitting in the doorway, pushing his feet through the dirt to make shapes and singing to himself. The sound came closer and became ever louder until it took over the world around him. His feet stopped moving in the dust and he stopped singing to listen. The terrible sound reached its peak directly above him, and a terrifying roar of engine mixed with the chat-chat-chat-chat of heavy machine gun fire forced him to cover his ears as a wave of down-blasted heat and sound pushed him over and back into the house.

Unhurt, he got back to his feet and watched silently, petrified with amazement rather than fear. In the street people were running and screaming as the helicopters sprayed the village with gunfire and dropped improvised bombs that exploded amongst the houses and traffic. A bomb landed at the foot of the hill towards the centre of the village and flames began to jet madly out of a bombed house. Emmanuel watched as the fire snatched at anything that would burn until all the cars at the bottom of the street were on fire. Between the burning vehicles he could see bodies smouldering in the road.

Emmanuel did not cry, but looked around with increasing wonder as the guerrillas recovered from their initial shock and shot into the sky with their AKs. The men didn't fire wildly like the teenage guerrillas he had once seen on an impromptu firing range on the outskirts of the village. Those boys had fired from their waists and emptied their magazines in seconds, splashing bullets everywhere and hitting everything except the old tin cans and bottles they had set up as targets. These men held their AKs tight to their cheeks, crouched with their knees bent for balance, and sent up short bursts of intense automatic fire just before the helicopters flew immediately over them. The fighters were the bravest men he had ever seen, they were calm and not running around, and although he was so young Emmanuel could understand what they were trying to do. They were aiming in front of the helicopters, hoping the machines' speed would carry them into the stream of the bullets. He was impressed by the fighters' logic, and mentally filed away his new-found knowledge of how to fire an AK at a helicopter.

Then, as suddenly as it had begun, the raid ended. The choppers turned out of the stream of bullets and banked steeply away from the village, picking up speed quickly until they were no more than small black spots heading back out over the northern hills. At first the village was quiet, and Emmanuel stood in the doorway watching the thick, oily plumes of black smoke rising from the wrecked cars and houses at the bottom of his street. The smell made his eyes sting. Then sound came back, and the acrid air filled with the moans of the injured and the wails of the bereaved, the shouting of men and the crackling of burning homes.

Emmanuel could not see how many villagers were dead and he would never find out. Neither could he find his aunt, and the old men who had been sitting on the steps had all disappeared. But the SPLA guerrillas who had stood in the street and fired their AKs at the helicopters were alive: they were gathering together all the remaining boys in the village. About twenty of them, including Emmanuel, were brought up to the top of the hill where one of the guerrillas slung his AK over his shoulder and spoke to them.

'This attack means the government will come again, but next time there will be soldiers and maybe tanks as well. And they will kill everyone.'

The boys shifted uneasily at the thought of soldiers coming to the village. Some of them started to cry; others shouted 'No!' But not Emmanuel—he had heard of massacres, and knew that such things could happen.

'Come with us and we will give you food and shelter,' the guerrilla continued. 'You will be safe from the government soldiers and you can go to school.' School was a magical word for Emmanuel. He was scared now and unsure what to do, but as he stood in the smoke and chaos of his bombed village he realized that something he had previously thought unobtainable was being offered; he would learn to read and write, and even to speak English. 'I was confused,' he recalled twenty years later, 'and when you are a child and you are told that you can go to a place where there is no war and go to school and become a better person—well, you agree. So I went.'

It was a decision that would change the course of Emmanuel's life. Because of it he would become a child soldier, a bona fide Kalashnikov kid in a chaotic war where sides and loyalties would change violently and often but seldom to his advantage. The SPLA had established a string of camps in south-western Ethiopia from which they supported and reinforced their presence in southern Sudan, but they were often overstretched and twenty years of warfare had depleted not just their ranks but the entire population of southern Sudan. As a result there were few men left for the SPLA to recruit. Boys were the next choice, and schools were a natural lure for them. The SPLA, conscious that the Arab north had higher levels of literacy which gave it natural military advantages, ran schools in its camps and discouraged outside aid agencies from providing teachers. In southern Sudan, the SPLA offered a child his only chance of an education.

In late April 1986, a week after the raid on his village, Emmanuel and the other boys made the 300-kilometre journey by foot and truck to the SPLA's area of operations in south-western Ethiopia. They were housed in a barracks that was part of a complex of camps and villages where up to a hundred thousand refugees, guerrillas and SPLA officials were living alongside Ethiopian citizens. A devastating famine had struck Ethiopia the year before—television images of it had led to that summer's Live Aid concerts in Britain and the USA—and Ethiopians were desperate to defend what scarce food and resources they had from the influx of

Sudanese. The Sudanese, however, had Kalashnikovs. Not surprisingly, tensions between the two communities were high.

It was in these conditions that the boys started their education, unaware that their maths and reading lessons were a means rather than an end for the SPLA. Sleeping with thirty other boys in a tin roofed dormitory, Emmanuel was amazed to find that as well as attending lessons he could also eat as much as he wanted.

'We were allowed to eat properly and grow strong. We were given food and learned to cook for ourselves at seven. We cleaned the houses and we also went to hunt—deer, antelope, any animal we could find, sometimes snakes and sometimes frogs. We hunted with sticks. Not the AKs—they weren't for hunting.'

AKs were for killing people, and after three months in camp the boys had their first intimations of what lay ahead. One morning they were taken out to a table under a tree by a guerrilla they had not met before and taught how to strip, clean and reassemble an AK47. It has only eight moving parts so the task is easy—Mikhail Kalashnikov had, of course, deliberately designed the gun so that hastily conscripted and illiterate peasants from Kazakhstan or Siberia would find it simple to operate. On this occasion the work was literally child's play, and within two hours Emmanuel and the other boys had learned by heart how to dismantle their AKs.

The military training was harsh, vicious even. Boys were beaten if they got it wrong, and were made to repeat exercises over and over again. The exercises themselves were simple: run at your enemy and shoot him. The SPLA officers found they had keen recruits who had no need of propaganda or indoctrination. They merely needed to answer the boys' questions about the war truthfully.

'We came from houses and places that had been destroyed. So we had bitterness in us already—we wanted revenge. The SPLA commanders didn't say, "Hate Arabs, they're bad", but when we asked, "Who burned our villages down?" we were told, "The Arabs did it." When someone asked, "My dad died. Who killed him?" the answer was, "Arabs." When someone asked, "Where are my brothers?" the answer was, "They have been taken into slavery in the north, by Arabs." So when they gave us an AK we were going to want to fight. We were told the stories about the Arabs, but we were the ones who decided to hate them. If you are a child you develop such anger that when you are going to fight you forget that you are a baby.'

But they were indeed not much more than babies, and as a loaded Kalashnikov weighs nearly four kilograms many of the boys struggled with the physical demands of being a child soldier in the SPLA. Twenty years later Emmanuel wondered not just how he could have fired such a big gun but how he even managed to pick it up and carry it into combat. 'I don't know how I lifted the AK when I was tired—it was so heavy.'

Boys also struggled with the psychological pressures of military discipline. Separated from their parents, with little or no emotional support and under constant pressure to be adults rather than children, they would often break down in tears. In these situations the drawbacks of arming children with AKs would become apparent. Even when fully trained they did not always understand just how deadly their AK was, and Emmanuel would see boys lose their wits under the pressure—to devastating effect. 'Boys went mad in the training camps, and started firing their AKs. I saw one of our commanders killed that way. A boy sprayed around with his AK and we all dived to the ground, and when we got up the commander was dead.'

The training went on, as the SPLA was desperate to bring its fighting numbers up to strength. In the late 1980s the movement was increasingly split. One faction wanted to continue fighting for a federal Sudan in which the south had autonomy and was not subject to the harsh Islamic Sharia law, but had a place in the national government in Khartoum; the other faction argued for complete separation and an independent southern Sudan. While this argument rumbled on in the top ranks of the SPLA, the trainee fighters were pushed even harder. Emmanuel would strip Kalashnikovs time after time. In firing drills he would be forced to parrot the different positions of the steel fire selector lever on the right-hand side of his gun: all the way up for safety on, one click down for automatic fire, two clicks down for semi-automatic. He learned that the trigger of an AK must be pulled back gently because it comes back further than triggers on other rifles before it fires; and when it does fire it can take you by surprise, forcing the bullet off target.

Emmanuel was nine years old when he first went into combat with his AK—not against the Sudanese government, but as part of an impromptu and unofficial children's war against a nearby Ethiopian village that suspected the SPLA children (correctly, as it turned out) of stealing their livestock. Emmanuel and his friends would sneak into Ethiopian civilian areas and take chickens, goats and even cows when they could. On returning to the safety of the camp they would quickly slaughter and eat the livestock. On one occasion they had just killed a cow when word reached them that enraged Ethiopian villagers were approaching the camp to search for their animal. The boys quickly buried the beast, then sat upon the mound with their AKs on their laps as the Ethiopians walked by.

The Ethiopian villagers were out-gunned, but a week later they came back with AKs and shot up the boys' section of the camp. Emmanuel joined hundreds of other boys for an emergency meeting on the evening of the attack. Tempers were high, and the boys decided to retaliate. 'They had started a war. Okay, that was fine—we had all learned what to do, and we knew how to fight. There were over a hundred thousand in our camp, so there were many young children ready for the attack. We had a few Kalashnikovs and some stones and sticks. That was enough. We were very angry and we weren't scared. We had never been into battle before so it was a bit like a game for us, like playing at being soldiers. We captured their village in an hour. We chased them out and then burned their houses down. Some of us were killed, but we had won—we had chased them away.'

In a startling exhibition of just how effective even small boys with automatic weapons can be—of how utterly the Kalashnikov can change the social order—a whole village had been laid waste by these children. Emmanuel was hooked. 'The gun had made me a man. Or it made me feel like a man. I knew people would do what I said, because I had an AK. With an AK47 you can get food, respect, anything you want. Even when you are nine years old.'

Within months of the fight against the Ethiopians Emmanuel was going into battle proper as the SPLA aided the Ethiopian regime by attacking rebellious villages. The SPLA did not favour the muffled night-time approach followed by a devastating AK firefight that had been employed so effectively by the Vietnamese against petrified GIs. Preferring much more direct tactics, the Sudanese fighters would launch themselves in waves at an enemy. The first wave was made up of children, often as young as seven or eight, who were sent ahead to run through the minefields—the SPLA's logic being that a boy is less likely to set off a landmine as he weighs less than a fully grown soldier. Behind them came older children carrying Kalashnikovs, and then another wave ready to pick up the weapons of the fallen. Sometimes Emmanuel was sent into battle in the third wave: 'We were sharing guns. You ran into battle carrying some magazines and stones and hid behind the person in front. He shot, and then you both ran ahead again. If he was killed you picked up his Kalashnikov. When it was our turn we just shot "Bam! Bam! Bam!" with our AKs. That's how I went to war.'

As he gained experience and seniority Emmanuel was given his own Kalashnikov, and he fought sporadically as the SPLA took its war with the Sudanese government back across the border and into the homeland. Despite the death and destruction he saw around him, and the high casualty rate, he and his fellow boy soldiers maintained an attitude towards war that was essentially child-like. 'It was like a game with toy guns, but when the war begins you can put the gun down and run away or you can pull the trigger. Once you've done that you will come into battle again because you will be experienced with the gun, and it will pull you in. You'll even try and get to the front—that's what an AK can do to you. It makes you think that no one can touch you. It makes you do dangerous things, take more risks when you go into battle. Once you've fired an AK47 you become brave. If you are not careful the gun sends you into battle.'

The SPLA used its bases in Ethiopia to reinforce and supply its occupation of much of southern Sudan, and gradually it gained territory. Since 1988 there had been an even more extreme government in the north: the National Islamic Front (NIF) (which from 1991 played occasional host to Osama bin Laden) which had renounced possible peace negotiations and recommitted itself to complete victory in the civil war. In 1990 the Iranian government bankrolled a NIS deal with Communist China that replaced the Sudanese government's entire stock of Kalashnikovs with brand-new Chinese models. By 1991 more than 4 million people had been displaced and 2 million killed in the southern Sudan alone and, disastrously for the SPLA, Mengistu Haile Mariam was overthrown in a coup in May. The new Ethiopian government was not well disposed to what was virtually an army of occupation on its western borders, and the SPLA were forced to return to Sudan. Without their Ethiopian support lines the SPLA gradually lost Sudanese territory, and within three years it was pushed back right to the southern border.

At this point inherent tensions in the movement came to the surface and the SPLA split between a mainstream faction committed to a federal Sudan under John Garang and a breakaway SPLA United faction lead by Reik Machar. After Machar unsuccessfully attempted to topple Garang his troops fell back for support amongst the mainly Nuer population of the Upper Nile and he established his headquarters in Waat, close to the Kenyan and Ugandan borders. Emmanuel stayed with the mainstream SPLA and walked over 800 kilometres to new positions in the hills near Juba, the traditional capital of southern Sudan and then under government control. Garang's forces had little heavy artillery and no air power but they were Kalashnikov-rich, and he planned to take the town by unleashing his regular guerrillas and a wave of child soldiers in an attack codenamed Operation Jungle Storm. Emmanuel was confident on the eve of battle: 'I wanted to go into battle with my AK. I was brave and I wanted to fight.' But even Kalashnikovs cannot guarantee victory, and although Jungle Storm started well it ended disastrously.

In June 1992 SPLA commandos forced their way into the centre of Juba and captured the NIF military headquarters for the whole of southern Sudan. Emmanuel and thousands of other SPLA child soldiers on the edge of Juba were instructed to run at the minefields that defended the government positions. At first the attack was a success and the SPLA began to advance into the centre of town in support, but the Sudanese government, which still held the Juba airbase, was already reacting.

Within a day of the assault Lieutenant General al-Bashir, joint leader of the NIF, flew into Juba personally and government aircraft and tanks followed him. It was enough to turn the battle, and as the SPLA attacks spluttered out al-Bashir unleashed what was, even by Sudanese standards, a frenzied reign of terror. Surrendering SPLA guerrillas were shot down in the street and civilians massacred in an outburst of killing and torture; the surviving southern Sudanese fled in disarray. For Emmanuel, the children's panic was as frightening as combat. 'When a child loses a battle he just runs away. You throw down your AK, you throw anything away. And then you cry like a baby. You cry for your mother. It is hard to convince a child to fight again if he has been defeated in war.'

Along with four hundred other boys Emmanuel turned his back on the SPLA and attempted to walk back to Tal in the Upper Nile. It was a desperate trip across vast tracts of minefield and scrub. Boys were so hungry that they shot vultures when they came near and scrabbled for snails under rocks. In some cases they were reduced to eating the corpses of other boys who had died as they walked. And there were many corpses—hundreds had succumbed to hunger and lack of water. To avoid the madness and pain of dying of thirst boys put their AKs in their mouths and pulled the trigger. Others made smaller boys than themselves urinate in cups at gunpoint so they could drink the liquid. Emmanuel had been walking for three weeks and was on the point of collapse when he fired his AK at a vulture and missed. The shots saved his life: friendly villagers were attracted by the noise and he was taken to Waat and the headquarters of Machar's SPLA United forces. It was not his village, but he would live.

There were just seventy survivors of the walk, who would become known as the Lost Boys. They joined hundreds of thousands of other displaced southern Sudanese scattered across camps in Kenya and southern Sudan or sent to the Achol-pi, a United Nations settlement centre in northern Uganda that was home to twenty-four thousand Sudanese refugees. Fed and washed but still weak, Emmanuel found himself with a new uniform and Kalashnikov and enlisted in Machar's movement. But after the disaster at Juba and nearly dying on the terrible trek across southern Sudan Emmanuel had lost his delight in being a Kalashnikov kid, and he struck a morose figure around the camp. Emmanuel was on parade with his AK when he was spotted by British aid worker Emma McCunes, who was working for a Canadian charity called Street Kids. McCunes was closely involved with the Sudanese struggle—too closely, perhaps, as she had married Machar—and she supported the south's fight against the Khartoum government. Despite this support, McCunes was horrified to find that someone as young as Emmanuel was a front-line soldier. She not only asked him to leave the army but took him into her compound at Waat where she began to teach him English and supplied the extra food he needed to recover from the walk from Juba. Within a few months McCunes had become a surrogate mother to the boy who could not remember his real mother.

Despite McCunes' protection, when Waat was attacked Emmanuel, who still had his Kalashnikov, chose to fight. Resources were so scarce in southern Sudan, and bandits so well armed, that raids on livestock were as much a threat as the Sudanese army. Over the next two months Emmanuel went into battle several times against bandit militia. He was still only twelve years old, yet he had survived dozens of combat missions. Never mind whether this was through skill or luck—there was a limit to how long he could go on without being shot and McCunes decided he had reached it. Determined to get Emmanuel away from Waat before he was killed, in January 1993 she managed to put him on an NGO flight to Nairobi in Kenya. As McCunes approached the Sudanese guards Emmanuel bent double and sneaked on board behind other passengers whom she had tipped off. At the airport McCunes flirted with the guards who ignored Emmanuel as he walked past with no luggage or papers. In Nairobi she sent him to school and moved him into her city apartment, but within six months of arriving Emmanuel experienced more tragedy. One morning he was taken out of his schoolroom to be told that McCunes, who was five months pregnant, had been killed in a car accident. He had known her for only eight months.

Emmanuel now found himself living in hostels with other Lost Boys. But he also came under the protection of Peter Moszynski, a British aid worker and journalist and friend of McCunes who travelled throughout East Africa's conflict zones and beyond reporting back to the United Nations. Whenever Moszynski could get back to Nairobi he gave Emmanuel money and helped him stay at school, but at the age of thirteen Emmanuel was now effectively in charge of his own destiny.

As he adapted to a new life away from his AK, sub-Saharan Africa became increasingly dominated by it. The more wars there were, the more Kalashnikovs were needed; the more Kalashnikovs there were, the more wars broke out. Warfare led to economic instability, and hundreds of groups of men with little food and no prospect of employment were fair play for any charismatic leader or robber baron who could guarantee them an income on the back of their Kalashnikov. Since hungry and desperate men were abundant, it was the Kalashnikov that became the vital part of the deal. The AK47 moved from being a tool of the conflict to the cause of the conflict, and by the mid-1990s it had become the progenitor of indiscriminate terror across huge swaths of the continent. How could it be otherwise? AKs were everywhere, and their ubiquity made stability a rare commodity as even the smallest groups could bring to bear a military pressure out of proportion to their actual size. In this way a movement as relatively small, bizarre and violent as the Lord's Resistance Army, across the border from Sudan in northern Uganda, could maintain a vicious war that had been raging on both sides of the border since 1987.

Garang and Machar too could be vicious, and in their struggle against the Sudanese government and their internal SPLA civil war both had committed atrocities; but they did at least have rational military and political objectives. On the surface the LRA's struggle was, like many others in Africa, a war fought by a marginalized tribal people—in this case, the

Acholi people whose lands straddle the Sudanese-Ugandan border—against the dominance of central government. But Joseph Kony, leader of the LRA, was a millennial visionary with a murderous sense of divine mission whose only declared aim was the imposition of the Ten Commandments as Uganda's national law. The Acholi were the primary victims of the war that Kony and the LRA claimed to fight on their behalf. Although the LRA's fighting strength seldom rose above five thousand and at times fell as low as eight hundred, its Kalashnikovs coupled with a complete disregard for civilian lives had given rise, since 1987, to extraordinary mayhem and misery in the region. By 2005 twelve thousand people had died as a direct result of the war and thousands more from the ensuing disease and starvation. Another 2 million civilians had been made homeless.

When Kony lost men—which in his early days he did, as before mounting an attack his guerrillas formed up in the shape of a crucifix, carrying burning torches, which made them easy targets—he simply kidnapped Acholi children to replace them. Some twenty thousand had been taken in this way by 2005. Unlike the Lost Boys of the SPLA there was to be no escape for these child soldiers. They were trained not just to fight the enemy but to murder without question in support of the LRA's primary tactic, in fact its only tactic and ultimately its core strategy: unbridled terror.

Kony's Old Testament-inspired holy war was within a tradition of religiously inspired rebellions in the region. Kony regarded himself as Moses and like the Israelite leader he didn't expect to see the promised land that all the killing was supposed to bring. With no prospect of being held to account for his actions, Kony maintained an Old Testament attitude towards his enemies—arms, legs, noses and ears were all lopped off civilians who were deemed to have offended the LRA. Although terrified by the LRA attacks, the Acholi saw the kidnapped children who committed them as victims themselves. This put them in a unique bind: they needed protection from LRA attacks, but could not support government actions against their oppressors which increasingly amounted to a policy of massacre.

Because Ugandan governments had armed and supported the SPLA against the NIF the Sudanese government supported the LRA. Throughout the 1990s and into the new century the conflict switched back and forth across the countries' borders. As Emmanuel progressed from child soldier to refugee and then musician other Sudanese refugees were being shot or hacked to death by the LRA. In 1996 a hundred Sudanese were massacred when the LRA invaded Acholi-pi. When the LRA returned to kill again in 2002 the United Nations shut down the refugee camp permanently.

The LRA's fortunes fluctuated: sometimes they were successfully ambushed by government troops, and on several occasions LRA troops took advantage of government amnesties and gave themselves up. But with Sudanese-supplied AKs and vast expanses of jungle to disappear into the LRA were virtually impossible to beat conventionally. Applying the classic counter-insurgency tactic of denying a guerrilla movement a sea to swim in, in 1991 the Ugandans set up defence militias amongst the Acholi to resist the LRA. These militias were armed with bows and arrows, but bows and arrows are not effective against children with Kalashnikovs. Outraged by even token resistance amongst the native population, Kony instructed his men, and boys, to hack off the limbs of anyone even remotely suspected of using a bow and arrow. This punishment was applied ruthlessly to whole villages—men, women and children.

Finally in 2003 the Ugandan government replaced the bows and arrows with Kalashnikovs. The LRA's grip on Acholi land weakened, and many of its fighters moved, across the border into Sudan. Although not the ultimate victory the government had sought, it was successful enough to reduce the terror and maiming. But it had come at a price—the Acholi population was now AK-empowered. And once the Kalashnikov is introduced into a society it is impossible to remove, like a virus that infects and reinfects its host: the illness it causes is conflict. In 1998 there were estimated to be 2 million AKs of varied provenance in Uganda; five years later the figure was doubled. In attempting to defeat the LRA, the Ugandan government had only created the conditions for more conflict.

Across the border in Sudan there appeared to be better news. In January 2005, after two years of negotiation between the Sudanese government and the southern SPLA, a treaty between the two sides was signed in Nairobi. The south would enjoy some independence, would not be subject to Islamic Sharia law and would have its own prime minister; however, the agreement was neither wide-ranging nor comprehensive enough to include the western Sudanese province of Darfur where the Sudan Liberation Movement (a separate organization to the SPLA) was fighting Kalashnikov-wielding pro-government militias who, throughout the winter of 2004–5, were inflicting genocide on the black African population. nonetheless the agreement appeared to offer a substantial step forward on the road to peace in Sudan and the Kenyan government as host of the talks arranged an evening of celebration on 9 January. On the bill was a twenty-four-year-old rapper from southern Sudan—Emmanuel Jal.

Emmanuel, who was now an established star throughout East Africa, had spent his late teens in Nairobi singing in gospel choirs organized by American evangelical churches and listening to American rap. He had developed into a strong singer, and by his early twenties was drawing crowds to street corners to hear him perform. As he grew more popular he began to write his own songs—songs about war and the child soldiers— and soon the crowds were willing to pay to hear him sing. To Moszynski's despair Emmanuel refused to take any money for himself—everything went to pay for hostels and lessons for his fellow survivors of the great walk from Juba, the boys who had shot vultures with Kalashnikovs and seen their friends starve to death. One song in particular was more popular than any other: 'Gua'—Nuer for 'peace'—was a plea for an end to war in the Sudan and a lament for the child soldiers. Moszynski, who now believed that Emmanuel was 'the voice of the voiceless', arranged a recording session in a Nairobi studio. The resulting single version of 'Gua' became a hit throughout East Africa.

Emmanuel sang 'Gua' at the signing ceremony, and it was so well received that he was asked to join northern Sudan's pre-eminent musician

Abdel Gadir Salim to record an album celebrating the ceasefire and treaty. But tensions were still so high that it was impossible for Emmanuel to visit Khartoum, so Gadir Salim's recordings were sent to London where Emmanuel over-dubbed his raps.

In London in 2005 Africa and war were at the top of the media agenda. The G8 were due to meet in Scotland halfway through the year, and campaigns and pressure groups such as Make Poverty History would be using the opportunity to push the world's richest industrial nations into relieving the burden of debt upon the world's poorest countries. Western popular culture had claimed Africa's suffering as its own moral property ever since Bob Geldof's original Live Aid concerts in 1985 and it was hungry to be involved again: rock music in particular would be seeking to exploit any sense of relevance it could extract from the process. As early as the 1970s British punk rockers The Clash had worn the Kalashnikov symbol of German Marxist terrorist organization the Red Army Faction, better know as Baader-Meinhof, on their t-shirts (it was actually a Heckler & Koch MP5 sub-machine gun, but such was the iconic status of the Kalashnikov that they thought it was an AK). More recently British group Manic Street Preachers had achieved international success with 'Kevin Carter', a song simultaneously bemoaning conflict in South Africa and celebrating the glamour of being involved in it with the hook line 'Bang Bang Club AK 47 Hour'. War in Africa had become a commercial property for rock. Its defining images—the starving mothers and babies, the Kalashnikov-toting child soldiers—had become part of the process of selling records. For rock, these references were about creating radical atmospheres. And in 2005 from Live 8 to War Child—the music-based charity campaigning to alleviate child suffering in conflict zones—there was a lot of Kalashnikov kudos to be had by a lot of bands.

Being a hardened veteran of war, hunger and enforced migration before he was fourteen meant that Emmanuel Jal was potentially a very hot property in such an atmosphere. When Moszynski used his United Nations contacts to take Emmanuel to the Edinburgh meeting to inaugurate Make Poverty History his protégé was fêted by Fran Healey, the front man of British rock band Travis. Healey, transfixed by Jal's credentials, immediately insisted that he must play at the concert.

But Bob Geldof decided who played at Live 8, and when Emmanuel was introduced to Geldof at the same gathering it quickly became apparent that Geldof was not interested in putting an African ex-boy soldier on stage at the main concert in Hyde Park. Geldof told Emmanuel, 'You have to sell four million records to do that. If you go on stage at Hyde Park the Chinese will switch off their televisions.' It seemed that Emmanuel's very authenticity would make him an embarrassment: a man who threatened to take control of the narrative from the West and give it back to Africa, back to where the AKs were.

But unknown to Emmanuel Jal there was a mounting sense of unease amongst observers about the relentlessly white and anodyne nature of the rock acts that Geldof was booking: the concert for Africa didn't look very African. Geldof instructed Peter Gabriel, a musician with a reputation for working with 'world' music, to organize an alternative British Live 8 concert at the Eden Project in Cornwall, where various African artists could play. Many of these artists came from a culture where the Kalashnikov was king, and they could all give convincing reasons why small arms control should be at the top of the world's priorities when it came to helping Africa.

Emmanuel played the Cornish gig. Rightly or wrongly, he regarded himself as the personification of the problems that Western musicians claimed to be addressing. More than that, he felt there must have been a reason why he had survived that walk through the bush when people around him had starved. Why, when children having tantrums had sprayed AK fire around his training camp, had he not been hit? Why, when he ran into battle with no gun at all, just waiting to pick up the Kalashnikov of the boy ahead, had nothing hit him? Why else should he have come through if not for a purpose?

With such self-belief he stole the Eden show and went on in early September to appear alongside Radiohead and Coldplay on the War Child benefit album. Like Emma McCunes' Street Kids, War Child was a charity dedicated to helping children in conflict zones, but it had astutely tapped into rock's need for Kalashnikovs. For the bands involved in the project Emmanuel was the real deal, an actual Kalashnikov kid who lent the album the kudos of actual conflict. In late September *Ceasefire*, his album with Abdel Gadir Salim, was released. This was an album about peace but the label, World Music Network, had no doubt about the iconic appeal of AKs and the cover showed the slouching silhouettes of two—presumably now unemployed—militiamen draping their arms James Dean-style on the AKs hung over their shoulders.

Increasingly, Emmanuel's experiences with an AK became a passport to greater media attention. He was invited to address a United Nations conference on the subject of child soldiers. In October the *New York Times* compared him favourably with American rappers as someone who really had been 'through the valley of death'. As Emmanuel turned his attention to breaking the American market Peter Moszynski stayed in England, where his north London flat was decorated with objects made from spent AK rounds and parts: amulets, charms, gadgets and small sculptures, little brass tokens of good luck and long life teased and beaten out from cartridges. He would show these to visitors and also, after rummaging through his chaotic filing system, some of the photographs he had taken over twenty-five years in Africa.

Amongst them were pictures of a displaced persons' camp in Sierra Leone in 2001—just one of the African conflicts to which Moszynski had been witness. A picture showed a nine-year-old boy whose right hand had been hacked off with a machete, another a girl who had lost both hands. At the back of one picture peacekeeping troops from the Organization of African Unity stood around with the latest Kalashnikovs, oiled and black with metal folding stocks. There was a sign in the camp that said, 'We must desist from the chopping of limbs for it will spoil our futures.' A crowd of children had gathered around the girl with no hands.

A half-dozen AKs were all that was required to stop the frenzy of limb-hacking that had overtaken these unfortunate people. There were no rock stars around to exploit the quiet business the AKs were doing. This scene would be no good for a video—it was just some bored-looking men in uniform chewing grass and occasionally changing guard. Moszynski had offered the pictures to the press but no one had been interested. Kalashnikovs doing good work doesn't sell newspapers or rock CDs.

At the end of 2005, after several clashes between the SPLA and government forces in southern Sudan, the treaty signed in January that year threatened to unravel.

A year after the London bomb attacks that killed 52 people on 7 July 2005 I sat over Turkish coffee in an Arab café with a famous British television war reporter. Through the window we could see Edgware Road tube station, where nine people had died when the ringleader, Mohammed Sidique Khan, had exploded his bomb. A few days after our conversation it was revealed that in 2001 Khan had visited Camp Hudaibiyah in the Philippines, a military base run by the Moro Islamic Liberation Front, a militant armed group fighting for an independent Islamic state in the southern Philippines. At Hudaibiyah Khan received a primer course in modern jihad or holy war, consisting of religious and political instruction, bomb-making techniques, physical fitness training and finally the instruction that was at the centre of the course and of life in the camp: Kalashnikov training.

Hudaibiyah was just one link in an international chain of camps and facilities that stretched from the Far East through Pakistan, Afghanistan and Iraq. The reporter had worked in Iraq, Palestine and the Horn of Africa and in a five-year career he had seen thousands of AKs in the hands of Islamic militants, government soldiers and militia. But his main concern on this summer morning was not the flood of Kalashnikovs throughout the Islamic world but what he regarded as the unfair treatment of British Muslims by the British popular press, which had been suggesting that they were a ready-made vehicle for violence and terror. As we sipped at our muddy Turkish coffee we did not touch upon the great irony that would become apparent to me as I looked deeper into the connections between south Asian jihadis and British Muslims: the fact that jihadi groups had exactly the same opinion of British Muslims as the tabloids, seeing their disaffected co-religionists as a potential reservoir of holy warriors. In a climate of growing suspicion and unease the reporter wanted the public to realize that young British Muslim men were not a fanatical band of terrorists intent on bringing down Western society but, like the majority of their countrymen, were primarily concerned with living peaceful lives. He talked about the demonization of young Muslims in Britain and the hysterical agenda of a British press more concerned with selling newspapers than with accurately reflecting what was happening in Britain's Muslim communities.

As an example he gave the case of Finsbury Park mosque in north London: 'It's presented as radical but it's actually a very large mosque. A thousand people worship there at a time, but all that's shown is one preacher outside on the street.' That preacher, Abu Hamza al-Masri, was jailed by a British court for eight years in February 2006 for incitement to racial hatred and murder. Egyptian by birth, Hamza had moved to Britain to study in 1979, but after rediscovering his Muslim faith he had become a firebrand preacher of jihad who was forced to give his sermons in the street after the mosque authorities banned him from preaching inside. Abu Hamza's appearance—he had lost both his hands and an eye clearing Russian landmines in Afghanistan, and was equipped with hooks and an eye patch—coupled with his emotive technique made him a popular target for the British press, who would regularly gather to hear his denunciations of the West made from within a protective ring of British policemen. Events outside the Finsbury Park mosque could seem like a circus, but Abu Hamza was no clown and, like other Islamicist militants, he saw the Kalashnikov as the main weapon of that jihad. Behind the farcical scenes on the street there had been very serious activities in the mosque.

'What about the rumours of AK47s in the mosque?' I asked the television reporter.

He put down his coffee and sighed. 'Yes,' he admitted. 'Incredible, really, but I don't think they were a real danger. It's more what the Kalashnikov means to these people. In the Middle East the gun represents resistance—that's why it's attractive to Western extremists. For young Muslims who are exposed to jihadi ideas, holding an AK47 links them with a whole array of fighters in Palestine, Afghanistan and Iraq and with Al-Queda. That's what the Finsbury Park mosque Kalashnikovs were about. I don't think anyone was ever seriously going to walk through central London with an AK47.'

On 20 January 2003 a police raid on the mosque revealed a store of weapons, stolen credit cards and passports hidden behind a polystyrene ceiling tile in the basement of the mosque. No Kalashnikovs were found, yet British Muslims later told police that there had been at least one AK on the premises in the late 1990s. British intelligence was convinced there were AKs in the building because they had at least one informer within Hamza's organization throughout the period in question. Indeed, British intelligence had allowed Hamza's associates to attend courses in the Home Counties where British ex-servicemen trained them to operate AK47s. This is an old intelligence tactic: fund and control a revolutionary group's activities—then you can close it down at a time and place of your own choosing. But British intelligence had misunderstood what the AKs were for. The training was not supposed to produce a cadre of urban guerrillas, but rather it was an initiation ceremony in which the AK was the central prop. The reporter was right: the AK47s in the Finsbury Park mosque were never meant to be used on the streets of London. Their purpose was to symbolize jihad to young British Muslims, and it was a technique that Hamza and the other British-based radicals had learned from Osama bin Laden, the master of organized Islamic war in the modern era, who relentlessly used the Kalashnikov as a symbol of his struggle.

Bin Laden first picked up a Kalashnikov on the Afghanistan-Pakistan border in 1979 where he was a key figure in Maktab al-Khidimat, an organization set up to channel Kalashnikovs and volunteers to the Afghan resistance via a network of camps on both sides of the border. The war brought Muslims from all over the Middle East and beyond to the bleak mountains of the Hindu Kush, and millions of AKs were imported to arm them.

The fierce warrior culture in Afghanistan predated the introduction of Islam, and its arrival merely served to increase and give a new justification for the mountain tribes' taste for fighting. The violent injunctions of the Quran found a perfect match in a culture of male hierarchy that was based on a system of honour through combat. Manhood was defined among Pashtoun tribes on both sides of the border by owning a rifle, feuds were settled with guns, justice was imposed by guns, a man's wealth was judged by the number of guns he had at his disposal and local politics were governed by guns. For hundreds of years the Afghan tribes lived in relative isolation, free to kill each other but having little effect on the world beyond their mountainous borders. Then in the nineteenth century Afghanistan found itself at the meeting point between two great and ever-expanding powers, the Russian Empire spreading down from the north and the British Empire edging up from India.

Both powers would come to regret engaging such a merciless and hardy enemy on its own territory. When the British sent two and a half thousand troops north from India through the mountains to Kabul in 1880 the Pashtouns let them cross the border, then attacked them with an army of twenty-five thousand. A thousand British died and the remainder of the attacking force fled, leaving their rifles behind them. A hundred years later the Soviets, who in 1979 invaded Afghanistan, ostensibly at the invitation of the communist government which was facing major internal opposition, had a similar experience of accidentally arming a fearsome enemy with better technology than they already possessed. But unlike the British they stayed to face the consequences in a ten-year war, which cost 15,000 Soviet lives and turned much of the country into a lawless killing ground. The USSR gave the Afghan government thousands of AKs from 1979 onwards, but although the government was communist many of its soldiers, unwilling recruits from the hill tribes, were not. These troops took the first opportunity to run away and join the anti-government Mujahadeen guerrillas, and they took their AKs with them. If a Russian convoy was captured it resulted in even more AKs being released into Afghan society, and when the CIA began to send shipments of AKs through Pakistan the region found itself with the highest concentration of Kalashnikovs in the world.

Many of the AKs that reached Afghanistan and Pakistan's border zones were very old—Chinese model 56s or even original Russian AK47s—but they were still mechanically sound and because they were so simple they needed only minor renovation to make them good for another thirty years of use. Even the Afghan landscape was changed by the Kalashnikov. Following the Mujahadeen's early successes in attacking military convoys the Russians cleared away vegetation for 300 metres—the effective range of an AK47—on either side of all main roads, pushing trees and bushes over with tanks and bulldozers or spraying them with defoliant agents. It was a public and shaming admission of Soviet vulnerability to what they had previously thought of as their own gun.

Across the border the Pakistan government failed to see the threat to its own security that was implicit in the conflict. Enjoying the full support of a US government that saw militant Islam as a convenient stick with which to beat Soviet communism, Pakistan responded to the invasion by channelling huge quantities of weapons through Afghanistan to the various Afghan factions. Untraceable and cheap, hundreds of thousands of Kalashnikovs found their way to the North-West Territories border region. Since the creation of the state of Pakistan in 1949 this region had never been under the full control of central government, and by inundating it with Kalashnikovs the government ensured this would remain the case for decades to come. When government forces enter the region they are tolerated as long as they do not enforce its authority; so naturally there is no central authority and each tribe or warlord makes sure they have enough armed men to control their area and protect it against their neighbours. By seeking to beat the Russians Pakistan's Inter-Service

Intelligence Agency (ISI) turned the North West and tribal territories into an armed camp, giving birth to what their own officials would ruefully call the Kalashnikov Culture.

As the war raged, hundreds of thousands of refugees came into the country and were settled in shantytowns in and around the cities of Peshawar and Quetta. Outside the immediate control of the Pakistani police and the ISI, competing Kalashnikov gangs ran these communities. Regular gun battles became a deadly fact of life in camps that became a microcosm of north-western Pakistan's wider disarray. Afghan fighters flitted backward and forwards across the border as it suited them, and on the Pakistani side a cottage arms industry developed as tinsmiths discovered their relatively simple technology was perfectly adequate for repairing Kalashnikovs. Some Pakistani towns and cities became in effect giant arms bazaars. Sakhakot, 65 kilometres north-east of Peshawar, was packed with shops selling AKs and workshops where damaged guns were reconditioned. A wide range of Kalashnikov variants were available— AKMs, AK47s, AK74s,—and because there was a glut they were cheap. In 2002 an AKM cost $200, an AK74 $250. Some enterprising tinsmiths even began to produce their own AKs from spare parts. These were good enough to attract the attention—and admiration—of Mikhail Kalashnikov, as he had told me when I visited him. But the general's invention had been intended to help Soviet soldiers; the inheritors of his mantle, in the dark workshops of Sakhakot, were committed to killing them.

When the Soviets finally withdrew from Afghanistan in 1989 the Kalashnikov's influence had spread far beyond Pakistan's border region and as far south as Karachi, the country's capital and main port. The city was used by the ISI as the central point in its distribution operation; from there the guns were meant to go straight to the camps on the border, but over a decade thousands had disappeared via corrupt local officials into the city's web of drug runners and gangs. Once inside the city the guns created their own momentum of violence and in the early 1990s the tense atmosphere between the city's Punjabi and Sindhi communities exploded into open warfare, forcing the government to send the Pakistani army on to the streets.

These drastic measures brought Karachi under control, but the border regions were still run by regional warlords, jihadi groups and drugs gangs, all of whom were masters of their own turf. Yet rather than learn from this ceding of national territory to armed gangs the ISI repeated its mistake and throughout the 1990s set up camps to channel more Kalashnikovs to guerrilla groups such as Jamaat-e-Islami, who were all fighting to expel Indian occupation forces from the disputed region of Jammu-Kashmir. In arming such groups the ISI gave away control of Pakistan foreign policy, for it would be impossible ever to have full peace with India while Pakistan was home to thousands of Islamic militants who were dedicated to unstinting war with India. In 1999 Hussain Muawia, of the guerrilla group known as Karwan-e-Khalil-bin-Walid (KKBW), called on Muslim youth to 'pick up the Kalashnikov unitedly'. He went on to announce that the KKBW would 'destroy the USA' if it acted against Osama bin Laden. More alarmingly for Pakistan's backers in Washington, he claimed he had the support of Pakistan's army in his plan to liberate Kashmir. The Kalashnikov had blurred the boundaries between illegal and legal, friend and foe. Perhaps now CIA officials regretted the decision to support the Mujahadeen in Afghanistan.

One Kashmir liberationist group in particular benefited from this situation. Lashkar-e-Taiba was funded, like many other jihad groups, partly by Saudi interests and direct payments from Osama bin Laden; it also received support from the ISI, who made sure it was well equipped with Kalashnikovs. Lashkar-e-Taiba was not a genuinely Kashmiri group—its founders were all Pakistani, and it recruited fighters from as far afield as Indonesia and Algeria. Its main base was near the town of Muridke near Lahore, originally established, with Saudi money and ISI assistance, during the Afghan war to train guerrillas to fight the Soviets. This massive camp covered more than half a square kilometre and contained its own mosque, carpentry and metal workshops, clothing factory, and houses and barracks for visiting jihadis and foreign religious students. Throughout the 1980s and 1990s it played host to annual conventions which attracted up to two hundred thousand militants who were exhorted to take up the gun. The walls were plastered with posters depicting a conjoined Kalashnikov and Quran, and the donation of funds to buy more Kalashnikovs was presented as a religious obligation for believers.

In the 1980s, before he was a fugitive, Osama bin Laden acted as chairman for many of the convention's theological debates; and in a reciprocal arrangement in the 1990s men from Lashkar-e-Taiba's armed wing, Markaz Da'wa Wal-Irshad, would train at Al-Queda camps in Afghanistan. After bin Laden went into hiding in the late 1990s he still addressed conventions at Muridke. Speaking by mobile phone, he would be broadcast live to meetings. A suite of rooms was maintained for him in case he should come down from his mountain hideout to wave an AK at the assembled throng, and he may have used these rooms in the 1990s. The ISI were unlikely to have stopped him: the Pakistani security services were so implicitly involved with Al-Queda and the other jihad groups that they never seriously undertook the CIA's injunction to track bin Laden down. In fact, American security officials are now convinced that the ISI helped bin Laden evade capture on several occasions.

A military coup led by General Pervez Musharraf in 1999 promised to restore order to Pakistan, but it proved impossible in a country where the Kalashnikov dominated life. The repercussions would go far beyond Pakistan's borders; Mujahadeen bases in Pakistan would become the seedbed of Al-Queda and the Kalashnikov the symbol of a new and victorious Islamic militancy with worldwide ambitions.

When bin Laden founded Al-Queda in 1988 he was careful to maintain the link with the Kalashnikov. Omar Bakri Muhammad, the Syrian cleric and so-called house philosopher of Al-Queda, famously claimed that 'Western culture is nothing more than entertainment.' Clearly this was a denunciation; yet although Al-Queda advocates a form of the reactionary Islamic observance known as Wahabism, which rejects innovation and seeks to turn the clock back to the seventh century, it is not a philosophically moribund movement. Al-Queda is adept at using the techniques of its enemies.

The entertainment and manufacturing industries that drive Western consumer economies are marketed, sold and understood through a series of global brands. Once it had acknowledged the power of these brands, it was only natural that militant Islam would develop its own. After twenty years of war in the Middle East the Kalashnikov had become an icon of the Arab struggle against Zionism and Western imperialism. To develop it into the symbol for jihad was merely a matter of an astute marketing campaign using television, the very tool that Western society regarded as its own.

It is clear to a Western audience brought up on a diet of near constant television that bin Laden, a man of medieval outlook in his religion and politics, is an artful manipulator of the modern media, an expert at using the tools of the enemy. From 1998 onwards he sent video messages to his supporters, which, once released to international television stations, brought him a worldwide audience. The Al-Queda leader made a point of being accompanied by a Kalashnikov when he was on screen but not always the same Kalashnikov: bin Laden's film career has seen him appear alongside a range of AK variants. In one early appearance he stands with his bodyguard, clutching a folding-butt AK that was possibly taken from the Soviet army ten years before. In another he appears with a snub-nosed AKS-74U, a sub-machine gun made at the Tula ordnance factory and designed for Special Forces fighting in confined urban settings. The presence of the AKS-74U may have been intended to warn any Special Forces planning to launch a mission to capture or kill him that he was ready to take them on. It was a timely message, for by the turn of the millennium bin Laden was possibly the most wanted man in the world. Following the Al-Queda attacks in August 1998 on US embassies in Tanzania and Kenya that killed 224 (including 12 Americans) and injured 4000, and a suicide attack on the warship USS *Cole* in Aden in October 2000 that killed 17 servicemen and injured 39, the US government had put a $5 million bounty on his head.

Apparently undaunted by the USA or its money, in the summer of

2001 bin Laden released his fiercest Kalashnikov propaganda video yet. A nine-minute-long paean to the dedication and fighting prowess of the man and the movement, it has two stars: the leading man is bin Laden himself, but if this had been a Hollywood production equal billing would have gone to the Kalashnikov. Guerrillas line up to shoot at pictures of former US President Bill Clinton, and children are shown carrying AKs as bin Laden gives thanks to God for the success of the USS *Cole* attack. Bin Laden is dressed in white, the uniform of an Islamic redeemer, and the film implies that the redemption will be brought about with a Kalashnikov. Strange, perhaps, given that Al-Queda's greatest successes so far had been achieved with bombs, but, as we have seen so often, the AK offers a unique proposition: you don't need to fire it to achieve your ends.

By 2001 bin Laden's propaganda had been so effective that training with an AK became a rite of passage for any prospective jihadi. In Britain there was the added *frisson* of using a weapon that was illegal to own. Men like Hamza who had been to Afghanistan were immersed in Kalashnikov culture, and when they sought haven in Britain in the 1990s they brought the gun with them. The Finsbury Park mosque had accommodation for up to two hundred people and as well as British Muslims there were foreign visitors: Arabs and Pakistanis, veterans of the conflicts in Afghanistan and Bosnia, who could speak compellingly of their experiences and the effect of an AK on the body of an 'infidel' soldier. For young men from the Asian suburbs of outer London or the drab and impoverished terraced streets of Yorkshire and Lancashire, such stories offered a compelling glimpse of a far more fulfilling life. And at the heart of all the stories was the gun.

The atmosphere of brotherhood and secrecy created among the trainees at Finsbury Park had repercussions around the world. Richard Reid, the shoe bomber who was overpowered by passengers when he attempted to explode a device on a US-bound American Airlines passenger jet in 2001, was one of those taught to fire an AK47 underneath the mosque. As well as receiving AK training at Camp Hudaibiyah, Mohammed Sidique Khan also attended Finsbury Park. So did Zacarias Moussaoui, the French Moroccan convicted in the USA in 2006 for his alleged part in the 9/11 attacks.

At 1 a.m. on 30 April 2003 another graduate of Finsbury Park's Kalashnikov classes, twenty-one-year-old Omar Khan Sharif, attempted to enter Mike's Place, a popular music bar on Tel Aviv's buzzing Mediterranean beachfront. Alongside Khan was Asif Hanif, twenty-seven. The men were dressed casually, like hundreds of other clubbers in the Israeli city's beachside area, yet something about their appearance and manner alerted the security men and they were stopped at the bar's entrance. An argument started and Hanif, realizing he would not be able to get inside the bar, pulled a cord beneath his shirt to detonate the bomb strapped to his waist. Simultaneously Sharif pulled his detonator, but the second bomb failed to explode. In the smoke and confusion caused by Hanif's bomb Sharif panicked and fled across the beach, dropping his bomb in the sand as he ran. Hanif had been killed instantly. Sharif's body was found washed up on the beach three days later; the Israeli police claimed he had accidentally drowned as he fled.

If Hanif had not been stopped at the entrance his bomb would have caused almost unimaginable carnage in the packed bar. Because he was, the night had a relatively low death count. Although over fifty people were injured, only five, including the bombers, were killed and the attack on Mike's Place would have been forgotten quickly if the bombers had been Palestinian. But they weren't. Within a few days of the attack the Israelis produced passports that proved both were British-born Muslims who had entered the country deliberately to become suicide bombers. Hanif was from London and Sharif was an ex-public schoolboy from Derby. This was the first instance of Hamas, the militant Islamic resistance group that claimed responsibility for the attack, using a European bomber to attack an Israeli target; and the first time, it was claimed by the British press, that British nationals had volunteered to be suicide bombers.

Eleven months after the attack, Hamas released a video. Filmed at an apartment block in Gaza City in the weeks before the attack on Mike's Place, it featured Hanif and Sharif dressed in camouflage combat fatigues and green scarves printed with the Arabic logo of the Qassam Brigades, the military wing of Hamas. It was a martyrdom video, a televised suicide note that Palestinian bombers leave to be released after their missions have been accomplished—yet this video did not feature the usual gaunt young men from Gaza or the West Bank. Plump-faced and white-toothed, Hanif's and Sharif's appearance immediately declared them not to be Palestinians. The men's uniforms had never seen combat; they hung baggily on their bodies and still showed the fold marks from their box.

Hanif talked, apparently happily, into the camera. 'I am doing this for the sake of those people who would like to distribute this among Arabs to show how sick [of the situation] we really are.' Yet for all his rage it would be hard to imagine a more unlikely-looking pair of jihadis, and indeed the clip would have verged on the comic—at one point a mobile started to ring as Hanif was speaking—if it were not for two objects that gave the Hamas production its menace and genuine terrorist credentials: both men were holding AKs across their chests. Once more the camera had picked up on the sublime design of the AK—the curve of the magazine, the parallel lines of the barrel and the gas tube.

Other Islamicist groups followed bin Laden's lead and began to record their actions on video. Muslims increasingly had access to films of sometimes horrifying violence sneaked into Britain, France and Germany by imams and veterans of the wars in Algeria, Bosnia, Chechnya and Kashmir. In Britain the main audience for these films was not among the comfortable Arab and Iranian émigrés in the Middle Eastern cafés of central London where I drank Turkish coffee with the famous war reporter, but in the south Asian communities of what was once the industrial North. If I wanted to talk to the young British Muslims who were being targeted as the next Kalashnikov generation I shouldn't be listening to Lebanese music on the Edgware Road but travelling to the Victorian terraced streets of Yorkshire and Lancashire where hundreds of thousands of Pakistanis had settled in the 1960s and 1970s. They had come to work in the textile industries that spread across both sides of the Pennines and from the moment of their arrival had encountered racism and discrimination. The indigenous population was both baffled by and antagonistic to an incoming Islamic culture that seemed unable or unwilling to accommodate itself to a society in which sexuality was commercialized and advanced age was not necessarly held in the highest regard.

As the cotton and wool industries waned the community turned in on itself, leaving the next generation in the paradoxical position of being ill at ease with the culture of rural Pakistan to which their parents still clung and yet resentful of the British society that still did not fully accept them as its own. Emotionally, intellectually and politically the second and third generation of British Asians were the perfect recruiting ground for any Islamic groups that offered salvation, dignity, purpose and a coherent explanation for their present plight—an explanation which blamed not them or their culture but a wider Western conspiracy against Islam.

To the jihadis Britain's young Asians appeared to be heaven-sent; not only a ready-made fifth column inside the enemy camp, but one that was already physically linked to the jihadis' bases in south Asia. Three-quarters of a million British Asians have relatives in the region, and thousands go back to Pakistan every year. Of course, the vast majority have no intention of going up to the tribal territories to join the camps, but the various jihadi groups that were now eyeing western Europeans didn't need thousands—just enough young men to blow themselves up on a train or a bus. If one or two of these returnees could be diverted each month, the jihadis would have enough men to take their campaign against the infidel to the streets of Britain. And what better way to attract the attention of a young man than with an AK47? Accordingly, the men who targeted Britain's young Asian males used the Kalashnikov as the brand identifier for their cause, and the gun proved to have a powerful pull on its target audience.

I found this out for myself in 2003 when I travelled to Leeds in West Yorkshire to meet two twenty-one-year-old cousins who, I had been informed by a contact in London's Asian community, had recently visited jihadi training camps. I met Abdullah and Rahim in central Leeds and took a bus with them to the run-down area on the edge of the city where they lived, close to Beeston, the Leeds suburb that was home to

Mohammed Sidique Khan. Both men were willing to talk to me about their experiences in the camps and the use of the Kalashnikov as a propaganda device in Britain, but only on condition that their real names were not used. 'Ever since the London bombings the climate has been very bad for young Pakistanis. We didn't do anything wrong when we were out there,' Rahim told me in his broad Yorkshire accent, 'no one in Pakistan tried to stop us, and Pakistan is supposed to be an ally of the US and the UK—but I still don't want the police to come looking for us. We could end up in jail or, worse, get sent to Guantanamo. Just for picking up an AK47.'

As we passed through the outskirts of Leeds the cousins disparagingly compared the area to Pakistan, which, although they had been born in Yorkshire, they clearly thought of as home. For Abdullah it was merely a depressing part of his way home. For Rahim it marked the division between believers and unbelievers. For me it made for a drab and unlikely backdrop to a story of propaganda, Kalashnikovs and, in the cousins' case, a close escape.

Rahim thought the only hope for their community was to turn back to their religion, to find meaning and dignity in the Quran. Abdullah was less certain. He knew things were wrong, but he wanted a way out that didn't require extremism or separation. It was a peculiar experience, almost comic, to hear such an intense debate on a bus, but events in London two years later would give the conversation a deadly seriousness in retrospect.

'Look,' said Rahim, 'wherever Muslims are being oppressed or killed, who is doing it to them? America every time.'

'But that's no excuse for suicide,' said Abdullah. 'It's against the Holy Quran.'

'And what else do our brothers in Chechnya have to resist with? AK47s and suicide bombs, that's all. The same as our brothers in Kashmir and Palestine.'

'How can you excuse suicide bombs?'

'How else can we fight the powerful?' replied Rahim. 'Using martyr operations against the Zionist isn't immoral—it's the only thing you can do.'

After half an hour on the bus and a ten-minute walk we entered Abdullah's terraced house and sat down to watch a video in the front room. Littered with tabloid newspapers, pizza boxes and computer games such as Doom and Counterstrike, it was no bin Laden's cave. The cousins were excited about watching the video, and I quickly realized it was caused as much by the vicarious thrill of seeing the AK in action as it was by the prospect of holy war. After Abdullah's eight-year-old brother had been ordered out of the room Rahim closed the curtains and pushed the video into the player. A series of lines and squiggles appeared on the screen before a jerky picture emerged, then disappeared completely before settling to reveal a dusty landscape.

A group of men jumped over a wall, then stood stiffly to attention. Their sleeves were rolled up to the elbows and each man was wearing black gloves. They held their AK47s a little in front of their chests. The men fell on to their stomachs and started to fire in short bursts at an unseen target, then got to their feet and started to run. They jumped over a row of obstacles made from oil drums and sandbags before flinging themselves to the ground, turning over and crawling on their backs under wire that had been pulled tight at knee height between wooden pegs. As they crawled, another man dressed in khaki fatigues appeared at the side of the assault course, crouched down and fired short bursts from his AK just above the wire. The men continued, propelling themselves forwards with a snaking wiggle of the spine and by digging their shoulder blades into the hard earth and pushing themselves onwards. When they had cleared the wire they jumped up and ran again.

The image switched to the interior of a concrete-walled building where the camera focused on another man. He too wore black, but had tied a green silk scarf around his forehead. There was Arabic script on the scarf and the man was looking directly into the camera. He spoke for five minutes and then the picture changed again, flickering and jerking on and off before it cleared to reveal a dusty road that stretched along the steeply sloping side of a mountainous valley. The place was rock-strewn and barren apart from patches of pine forest that followed the line of white road that worked its way up the incline via sharp corners and long stretches of straight slope. A pale blue winter sky was visible between the mountains.

The camera tracked back and forth along the road, and up and down the hillside. Whoever was operating it was searching for something. The picture went in and out of focus. 'Chechnya,' explained Rahim by my side on the couch. A white car was coming up the road from the valley floor. The camera followed it for a while, then turned its attention further up the road past a stretch of woodland that flanked the road for a kilometre. There it picked out two military trucks coming down the road. As they approached each other the car and the trucks disappeared into different ends of the forest. It was hard for our eyes to follow the vehicles between the trees; only the occasional glimpse of white paint indicated the car's upward progress, and nothing at all could be seen of the trucks. Then, at the point where the car going up and the trucks coming down must have crossed, a flower-burst of yellow flame edged with black smoke billowed out of the trees. Caught up in the flames were indeterminate scraps and black lumps that hurtled upwards and outwards as the woods were engulfed.

The force of the explosion crossed the valley seconds later. The picture wobbled and then jerked down to show the operator's black walking boots before cutting out. Then the picture came back. The sun was still in the sky and there was no sure sign of how much time had elapsed. The cameraman had moved across the valley to the site of the explosion and was standing in a blackened space by the road where the wood had been devastated for a radius of twenty-five metres. All that remained of the white car was an engine block that sat on the edge of a blast crater in the middle of the road. Both the trucks had been blown up the hill and lay in the charred and smashed woods above the road. One truck had come to rest on its side; the other was upright but it had lost its tyres and the driver's cab had been completely blown out. Around the truck, scattered on ground thick with pine needles, was a mixture of body parts, scraps of uniform and plastic bags that must have held the occupants' lunch. A crowd had gathered around the second truck—twenty or so men dressed in a mixture of Russian army blousons and jackets, patterned jumpers, jeans and trainers milled around the remains of the convoy. All the men carried AK47s.

The camera panned up to the top of the trees that ringed the site and zoomed in on a human torso caught high up in the branches. The torso was naked, and it was not possible to say if it belonged to a suicide bomber or to one of the Russian soldiers who had been his victims. The camera panned back down to the truck again, where the group of men had become very animated. There was no sound on the video, but the shape of their mouths and the way they were gesturing made it clear they were shouting with excitement. The men held up their AKs, and some of them danced. The cameraman went through the group to the back of the upright truck. Abdullah leaned forward on the couch to see what the men were looking at, then reached for a bottle of Coke and let out a gasp. 'Oh no, man!' The cause of the guerillas' excitement was revealed: they had found a survivor.

The Russian soldier was being pinned back against the rear of the truck by two guerrillas. He was no more than twenty-one. Fair-haired and blue-eyed, he had the slightly puggish face of a northern Russian. It was blackened by the explosion and smeared with blood. Apart from being stunned, it looked as though he had come through the ambush relatively unharmed. But if he had been saved from death in the truck by some higher power it was only so that he could suffer more now. The Russian soldier's face showed pain and terrified apprehension as he fought to free himself from the grip of his captors.

Another man, his AK slung over his shoulder and carrying a long knife, stepped forward and grabbed the prisoner's left ear to hold his head still. With the other hand he brought the blade up to the man's face and cut his nose off. The Russian kicked frantically against the gunmen who held him, but they maintained their grip on his arms and the man with the knife went in again to cut at his face. The camera fell back from them, allowing the man with the knife room to cut. The picture jerked and blacked out, and when it came into focus again there was absolute silence in the front room. A guerrilla was standing over the slumped and shaking body of the Russian, holding the muzzle of his AK against the back of the soldier's head where the blond hair was now matted with blood. The guerrilla smiled at the camera and pulled the trigger. The back of the Russian's head exploded, splattering the guerrilla's jeans with blood and brains.

'Fucking hell!' said Rahim.

It was a strange experience, watching scenes of horror from a far-off war in the front room of a terraced house in Yorkshire. There was a feeling of palpable excitement at the images of the Kalashnikov, yet at the same time a very British dislike of what they were seeing. The film was brutal, and hard to pass off as an example of a noble struggle.

Afterwards there was an uneasy feeling in the room, as if the cousins were embarrassed by what they had shown me. To break the atmosphere I asked them when they had first become aware of the Kalashnikov as the weapon of the jihad.

'It was 2001,' said Rahim. 'A black preacher called Abdullah Faisal came up to Yorkshire and we both went to hear him. He said, "We should train our young men to fight—to spread Islam by the Kalashnikov."'

Although Faisal had been based in London, I wasn't surprised to hear his name mentioned in the North. A Jamaican-born convert to Islam, he had been jailed for nine years in 2003 for racial incitement and soliciting murder of Jews, Americans and Hindus. Faisal was based at the Brixton mosque in south London—also used by Zacarias Moussaoui and Richard Reid—but regularly travelled to the Midlands and North to spread his message of violent jihad. He visited the Al-Madina Masjid mosque in Beeston, where Mohammed Sidique Khan worshipped (as did another London bomber, Shehzad Tanweer). Faisal had also preached at the mosque in Tipton in the West Midlands, from where Munir Ali, one of the 'Tipton Terrorists', set off to fight in Afghanistan in 2001 and was never seen again.

Implicit in all of Faisal's preaching—indeed its central message—was the need for young Muslim men to learn to use a Kalashnikov. 'Liberty', claimed one typical Faisal sermon, 'can never be achieved by democracy. The way forward can never be the ballot. The way forward is the bullet. Islam was spread by the sword. Today it has got to be spread by the Kalashnikov.' Faisal was a one-man advertising campaign for the AK47; he even suggested that Muslim mothers should buy their sons toy guns so they would be ready to pick up an AK when they were men. In exchange for martyrdom he offered seventy-two virgins and an eternity in paradise, but for a Western audience used to Madonna videos and computer games it was the Kalashnikov rather than the virgins that mattered.

Faisal was not alone in realizing that Western audiences were more attracted to brands than to promises of heaven. Rahim spoke at length about a preacher of Pakistani origin who had come regularly to a local mosque. For 'community safety' reasons Rahim said he would rather not name the preacher or the mosque, but he was happy to talk about the way he and his cousin were gradually persuaded that they should go to Pakistan and join the jihadi camps.

'This guy has since gone back to Pakistan. He said he had spent time across the border in Afghanistan, he claimed to have been a fighter, he made it clear that it was our duty to go out there and train to be fighters. His sermons were often like talks rather than speeches. He wasn't like some other preachers that shout at you—he was very calm. It was as if he was explaining something that had been obvious all along, but we'd just missed it before because we hadn't been paying attention—we'd been tricked by all the stuff that Western society throws at you.

'Going to fight was presented as the solution to a problem, so his talks would have titles like "Where to for Muslim Youth?" He would talk about some verse from the Quran and then we would have a question-and-answer session. He would start by asking something like, "What is your life here in the West like? How much respect do you get? How do the police treat you? You are treated like a second-class citizen yet you are a believer and the people who oppress you are unbelievers." Then he would move towards the solution: we had to find ourselves as good Muslims again and we had to fight. It was exciting, and when he said, "You have a duty to resist them, to fight the unbelievers if they make war on you", he really made me feel like I shouldn't be here and that the government was against our Muslim brothers around the world and it was our duty to help those brothers in any way we could—though the best way was to fight. We see it on the news anyway, but he made it clear for us: the West is committed to the destruction of Islamic civilization. If you doubt it, look at the government's support for the Zionists in Palestine or its support for India in Kashmir.

'He also talked about British society, about how depraved it was. And really, it was hard to disagree with him when he said, "They tell you that Muslims are against women because our sisters and mothers choose to follow the injunction to cover their heads and protect their modesty, but look at the pornography the Kuffas [Westerners] put on the television. On posters in the streets. In the newspapers. You cannot be a good Muslim and put up with this treatment."'

Rahim had been excited by the preacher's message from the very beginning, and gradually he became committed to the idea of going to a militant camp in Pakistan. 'We were going to Pakistan anyway, and I started to think seriously about going up to the tribal territories and joining a group, maybe even going into Afghanistan. I'll be honest—the prospect of fighting was very attractive to me. I was still a kid in some ways, and these guys were offering me a chance to play soldiers—but in a way that would make me a good man in the eyes of my religion. They would show us films of fighters in Pakistan. I could tell the fighters were just ordinary men—they weren't super-heroes or anything—but just by picking up an AK they had become different.'

I wondered if these videos were as startling as the video we had sat through earlier.

'They could be. Occasionally there would be a film of an attack in Pakistan or Afghanistan. But usually they were films of rallies. Typically there would be hundreds of men being addressed by a leader, and then the men would march up and down or just stand around and shout. All this happened to a soundtrack of exciting Islamic music, the real heroic stuff. It sounds daft, but I was more excited by them than the action films sometimes! Just seeing all those men with Kalashnikovs, thousands and thousands of them, it looked like our side in this war had our own special weapon and there were enough for anyone who wanted to join. It was easy to pick up the gun; we were really made aware of that. The preacher mentioned the Kalashnikov all the time. And he would link it with religion—make it seem like a holy thing to do. His catchphrase was "It is your duty to pick up the Kalashnikov." When I told him I was thinking of going back to Pakistan for a family trip with Abdullah he gave me the name of a mosque I should go to in Karachi and said, "While you are there you should learn some skills that can serve Muslims in the fight that is coming. It is your duty. Learn to shoot a Kalashnikov, because a war is coming between them and us. It doesn't matter if we want it—they have declared it already. They are fighting it in Palestine, in Jerusalem, in Chechnya and Kashmir. If you can, go to Afghanistan and learn to fight. God has given us Kalashnikovs. It is wrong not to use them." There were so many specific references to the Kalashnikov that eventually I became a bit obsessed about holding one.'

Rahim's cousin Abdullah had been less inclined to pick up the gun. 'I thought it was a bit mad. We live in West Yorkshire—I couldn't see what use Kalashnikovs were going to be to us. I mean, we weren't going to walk into Leeds firing them at people, were we? I thought there might be answers to our problems that were less drastic. I thought jihad could be a matter of personal conviction, of praying harder, not shooting at people. I was very excited about the trip to Pakistan, but worried that Rahim would disappear into a training camp and I would never see him again.'

Before the boys went to Karachi, Abdullah had spoken up at one of the meetings held by the preacher: 'Other Muslims live here and mix. Why can't we?' The preacher had replied, 'A Muslim cannot accommodate these people. And the people who say we can live amongst them are worse than Kuffas because they are telling Muslims a lie—the lie that we can mix, that we can all get along. We cannot get along with those who are untrue to

God. There are those who follow God and those who do not—you are either a believer or an unbeliever. "O you who have attained to faith! Fight against those unbelievers who are near you and let them find you adamant, and know that God is with those who are conscious of Him.'"

Abdullah responded, 'But that was written for a different time, for when Islam was struggling to survive in Arabia. It does not mean we should kill those who do not believe now.'

The preacher had paused before he replied, smiling at Abdullah. 'These words were the revealed truth and they are still the revealed truth. There are no different times for God. Unbelievers have always fought against Islam. Look around you. Who do you think started the fight? We must defend ourselves. It is our duty to God.'

'What if I don't want to shoot anyone?' asked Abdullah.

'There are many ways to fight—you don't have to pick up a gun. Do as you are planning to do, and go back to Pakistan with your cousin and find your religion again. And take your skills with you. Don't give them to the unbelievers. Give them to your own people. Make them strong.'

In April 2001 Rahim and Abdullah flew to Karachi. They spent a week with relatives, looking around the city. Everywhere there were soldiers with AK47s. Abdullah had never seen so many guns: 'They were all around, every kind of AK all around you in the street.' Rahim had been excited initially, but soon tired of wandering round and drinking tea and within a month of arriving he had decided to go to the federally administered tribal areas.

Their family warned them not to go. An uncle pointed out that the border was fierce and lawless, and having British passports would not guarantee their safety. But Rahim insisted and they flew to Peshawar where, after a few days in a hostel, they found positions as volunteers at what they were told was a refugee camp and medical centre near a small plateau high up the Tochi valley near the Afghan border.

'We took a seven-hour bus journey into the territories and just turned up at a camp,' Abdullah told me. 'It wasn't an impressive camp. Just a collection of low buildings and huts gathered around a hundred-metre square of baked earth. We were told it was run by the government, but the guards didn't wear the uniform of the Pakistani army.' They had scarves around their heads, wore waistcoats over their shirts and baggy cotton trousers that were gathered in at the ankle, and they had AKs slung over their shoulders.

They arrived with little more than a note that Rahim had brought from a mosque in Karachi—the same mosque that the preacher in Yorkshire had told them to visit. At the entrance a guard looked at the note with the haste of a man who couldn't read, then gestured the cousins to follow him. They walked across the compound and into the largest of the low buildings where they were introduced to the chief official in the camp, who served them tea and told them it was not a military base for fighters. It was supposed to be principally a hospital. But according to Abdullah it was rather more than that: 'Nearly everyone in the tribal areas carries a Kalashnikov, so everywhere looks like a military base: the markets, the schools, the hospitals. But this place was obviously something special. There were men there in perfect health coming through and staying for a day or two, then going over the border with fresh supplies. And at the back of the compound there was a dusty patch about the size of a football field facing the mountainside where people practised with their Kalashnikovs.'

Rahim and Abdullah were shown around the hospital at the centre of the camp. 'It was just made from rough breezeblock. Two rows of fifteen beds ran along two sides of the room. Each bed was occupied. Many of the men were about our age or older, but some of the men there could have been our grandads—guys who had been fighting for years. All of them had their AKs. It wasn't one of those situations where you get wounded and your weapon is handed on to the next man, because there was no shortage of guns. There was an absolute glut of AKs—it was incredible. They would lie in bed with their AKs, either hanging from bedsteads or lying by their sides.

'The camp leader told us most of the men in the hospital were fighters who had been injured fighting in Afghanistan,' remembered Abdullah, 'when they had clashed with rival smuggling gangs on the border or in simple feuds between tribes. The AK settles all arguments there—there are no police, so everything is done in the old way. Everything is a reaction, so if you are shot then your family will seek justice on your behalf, but there is no one to stop you being shot in the first place. When a round from an AK hits you it makes a mess. They had very few antibiotics or medicines, so if it hit a leg or an arm the chances are that you would lose a limb. If it's a body wound you have to be very lucky to survive. None of the fighters had body armour, apart from the big chiefs—and some of the men wouldn't wear it anyway. They saw it as unmanly, a sign of cowardice.'

It was, surprisingly, not Rahim, the warlike youth who was keen to pick up an AK and join the jihad, but Abdullah, unsure and ill at ease with guns, who fitted more easily into life in the camp, and he was employed as a clerical assistant in the office of the chief official. 'In the morning I would help with paperwork in the camp office. It only took an hour. Nearly all the patients were illiterate, and there were very few medical deliveries to check through against invoice. Occasionally the Red Crescent sent some supplies—clean sterile dressings and surgical gloves—but very little came from the government although I presumed they were paying the manager a wage. The everyday expenses of the hospital were met by the charity of local people and the militia who paid a little towards the care of their injured men. At least three times while we were there a truck came in the night and unloaded boxes of AKs. I don't know how many, but there were enough to keep four men busy for half an hour. They were put in a concrete bunker but I wasn't allowed down there.'

Rahim worked as an orderly on the hospital ward, and he had to wait a month before he got the chance to fire an AK. 'Officially we were not fighters and no one seemed keen to give us the opportunity. Maybe we had to prove ourselves. At first they were extremely suspicious of anyone who came in from outside unless they knew them, and they were very conscious that the Pakistani security services or the CIA might try and plant an agent in the camp.'

But one morning the opportunity came to do what Rahim had come to do: to train with an AK. 'The camp commander had a folding-stock

AKM he kept in a cupboard—he said it had been taken from a Soviet paratrooper. And he just came up to me after seven weeks and asked if I wanted to have a go with an AK. I remember his words exactly. He said, "Let's see what you're like." He took us out on the firing range at the back of the camp and taught us to fire it. I loved it. All the stuff I had heard in England came together in my head when he passed me the AK. I felt like a holy warrior there and then. The gun was perfectly balanced. I didn't have to make any effort to hold it—it seemed like a bit of me. But Abdullah didn't like it at all.'

Six thousand kilometres away from the experience now, sitting in a Yorkshire front room Abdullah laughed at the memory of his Kalashnikov training. 'I couldn't do it, and the guy just got cross with me. I was shooting everywhere—I nearly took their heads off!'

'He did,' agreed Rahim. 'So I asked for permission to take Abdullah out the next day and teach him myself. I was that excited. They said it was all right as long as another fighter went with us and we made a contribution to the cost of the ammunition.' Even on the second day, when Abdullah squeezed the trigger he had been so surprised that he fell over backwards. But after twenty minutes under his cousin's instruction he stopped falling over, and within an hour he was hitting the powdered milk tins they used as targets.

Cow and Gate would be the only victims of the cousin's jihad. 'I got scared,' Rahim admitted freely, 'and I realized that I didn't belong there. The promise of a Kalashnikov was one of the things that had lured me out, but I was growing up and once I'd had one in my hands I knew that I couldn't go into battle. And things were getting very scary.'

As the summer temperatures reached their hottest more men had come into the camp. Some were ill or injured; others stopped to pick up supplies, to have their AKs serviced and to catch up with the news.

'They were mainly Pakistanis,' said Rahim. 'But there were other men, from Bosnia and even Algeria and from elsewhere in Europe, who were going over the border to train in Afghanistan. We met fighters from all over. But I was confused by what they thought. They were all Sunni, like us, and they had no time at all for Shiites. I thought that was stupid. In England I had learned to respect what Shiites like Hezbollah were doing, resisting the Israelis, but I met one guy, a young Pakistani from a madrassa [Muslim theological college], who didn't even think they were Muslims. But how can you say the Shia in Lebanon are not good Muslims? Hezbollah drove out the Israelis. What have the Sunnis done to stop the Zionists oppressing our brothers in Palestine? The Jordanian royal family support Israel. The Egyptians support Israel. Anyway, they were very serious guys, extremely religious, and it made for a strange mix because you'd have a tribesman who'd never been out of the mountains sitting round a fire with a guy who knew what had been on MTV the week before! To be honest, I felt out of my depth.'

The talk would be about who was feuding with whom, when the next big arms shipments were going through, who was hiring gunmen. It was these groups with whom Rahim would sit and talk. But all of them said the same thing: the real fight was happening over the border in Afghanistan, the Taliban had created a caliphate—a microcosm in one country of what many militants hoped would be a future worldwide Islamic government.

Gradually the two cousins had become disenchanted with life in the camps, and when the chance came to go over the border neither of them took it. One morning Rahim and Abdullah watched a chain of men and mules leave the camp and pick their way up the mountain. Each man carried an AK, spare magazines, a bag of flour to make flat bread and a water flask; twenty minutes later they had disappeared into Afghanistan. A week later the two young men went back to Karachi, and in August they flew home to Britain, only weeks before the 9/11 attacks that would lead directly to the US invasion of Afghanistan.

They left behind a country that was inundated with Kalashnikovs and consequently almost impossible for even the harshest military dictatorship to govern. At a local level the police found themselves unable to impose the most basic law and order because anyone they might seek to arrest was invariably at least as well armed as they were. In Gujrat, a city with Al-Queda connections and an excess of AK ownership, the local police chief,

Munawar Hussain, was moved to declare in July 2004, 'I vow to eliminate the Kalashnikov culture from this district.' He would not be successful: a year later shops in the streets next to the city's cricket ground were openly selling Kalashnikovs.

In 2005 General Musharraf's Interior Minister, Moinuddin Haider, an ex-general in the Pakistani army, attempted to bring tribal areas and religious extremists in the major cities into line. His proposals were a direct challenge to Pakistan's Kalashnikov culture. No one apart from the security forces was to be allowed to carry arms in public, and madrassas and militant Islamic groups such as Lashkar-e-Taiba were to be banned from collecting money for arms, which Haider confirmed would be illegal even it was 'in the name of jihad'. In response the leader of Lashkar-e-Taiba, Hafiz Mohammad Saeed, said, 'This is an un-Islamic statement coming from a minister of the Islamic republic. We collect funds for the holy cause and display arms only in jihad.' A year later Kalashnikovs were still being openly carried on the streets of Peshawar and Karachi.

In 2006 the British press revealed, somewhat hysterically, the presence of Islamic training camps in Wales, the Lake District, the Yorkshire Dales, Hampshire and Berkshire. In many of the reports the extreme seriousness of the revelation was reinforced by the assertion that 'AK47 training' had taken place. However, as neither the press nor the British security forces produced any AK47s, there was no proof that they had existed. It didn't matter; the gun was used as a metaphor for Islamic militancy. In this way right-wing British newspapers such as the *Sun* and the *Daily Mail* found themselves engaged in the same media project as Osama bin Laden, Abdullah Faisal and Abu Hamza al-Masri.

I kept in touch with Rahim and Abdullah and was pleased to hear that they didn't go to Afghanistan to become jihadis. Rahim got a job in a bank, and Abdullah is a taxi driver. Recalling his time at the camp, Rahim said something which brought the Kalashnikov's symbolism and propaganda value for militant Islam into sharp relief: 'They train you to use a Kalashnikov, but what they really want you to do is blow yourself up on a bus or a tube. You don't need an AK for that.'

Neither Rahim nor Abdullah is involved with militant groups, and since the London bombings they have not watched any more holy war videos. And both of them are thinking of getting married. In their case, at least, the power of the Kalashnikov was not enough to lure them away from their compromised but ordinary lives amidst the irreligious Kuffas of West Yorkshire. But the gun would pull other young British men away from their homes and into a sandstorm of conflict and propaganda in the region. In 2003 the USA and Britain launched a war in the Middle East that would prove to be perfect territory for the Kalashnikov.

Ten months after the US and British coalition's invasion of Iraq in 2003, I was sitting in a heavily fortified barracks in south Baghdad with American soldiers of the 1st Airborne Division as a sergeant remembered the Mujahadeen he had encountered defending a vital bridge over the River Euphrates at al Samawah. 'We raced up from Saudi Arabia—the only Iraqis I saw had their hands in the air or they were dead. No one shot at us until we got to al Samawah on the Euphrates, where we were held up at a bridge by fierce AK fire. Our policy in a situation like that was to sit tight and call up firepower, air or tank. We didn't have to call anyone because three Abrams rolled up from behind us and crossed the bridge. Tanks usually make people get out of the way. It would certainly make me move—but not these guys. The Mujahadeen come out of the side streets on the opposite bank and started shooting at the tanks. They didn't have RPGs, just AKs—they were shooting at tanks with AKs!' I could tell from the sergeant's tone of voice that he still found it hard to believe what he had seen. 'They didn't even try and get out of the way. It was like they were on drugs, just standing there and firing off their Kalashnikovs at our armour. Eventually the Abrams turned their turrets and that was that. Boom! But I mean, shooting at tanks with AKs! That's something.'

The success of Desert Storm suggested to some in the Bush administration that conventional war was over. In the future, conflicts would be won with airpower and cruise missiles, leaving ground forces the simple task of rounding up the shell-shocked survivors. In this new age it seemed there would be little place for the AK47. What chance did a sixty-year-old assault rifle have against cruise missiles and Abrams tanks? Unconvinced that America's military might could overcome a gun that had long thrived in adversity and confusion, I had gone to Iraq to see for myself if this really was the beginning of the end for the Kalashnikov.

The Iraqi Mujahadeen at al Samawah had been destroyed, and the Americans swept over the bridge and continued their drive on Baghdad. It struck me, however, that this story did not spell the end of the AK's use in modern warfare but rather was a stark reminder of why it would never be out-of-date. In reality the war that was supposed to signal the end of its reign would give the Kalashnikov brand an even greater marketing push, establishing it for a whole new generation as the antithesis of US imperial power. It would also kill a lot of GIs.

Nobody knows for sure how many Kalashnikovs there are in Iraq; the American and British armies certainly didn't when they invaded. Their strategy was to beat the Iraqi army on the ground—which they accomplished with ease—with little or no planning for a war of resistance that might follow. They presumed, with what now seems to be astonishing hubris, that they would be regarded as liberators. Consequently, US military planners were surprised by the ferocity of the resistance that began within a few months of the official end of the war. Yet the briefest consideration of the country's recent history would have made it clear that, even if only a small proportion of Iraq's population rejected 'liberation', they had enough weapons to mount a fierce and punishing resistance. More importantly perhaps, the Kalashnikov was more than a weapon to the Iraqis: it had inveigled its way into every level of society, representing as it did manhood, power and, when necessary, violence.

Soviet AKs first arrived in the country in the mid-1960s as the Middle East divided along lines dictated by the Cold War: Israel and Jordan siding with the USA; Iraq, Syria and Egypt with the USSR. After Saddam Hussein took control of Iraq following an internal Ba'ath party coup in 1969 the country signed contracts with Communist China and Tito's Yugoslavia to import Chinese model 56s and the Yugoslavian Zastava M70B1 (itself a copy of the Soviet AKM). The stockpile of weaponry was expanded when the Iraqis began to produce their own Kalashnikov variants: the Tabuk, a copy of the Zastava M70B1, and the Kalashnikov-based al Quds (Arabic for Jerusalem) light machine gun. Both these guns were produced at the Iraqi state rifle factory outside Baghdad.

Much of the Sunni area of central Iraq is governed at an everyday level by tribal custom based on the authority of elders and sheiks, its traditions shaped by an ancient desert lifestyle that puts emphasis on family, the clan and personal ownership of an AK47. After the 2003 invasion and subsequent occupation, the number of AKs in circulation actually increased. The US military failed to guard Iraqi government arms dumps, and in March that year the entire stockpile of Iraqi army AKs disappeared into the population and the weapons were soon available for under $100 each.

This central massive supply of guns ensured that America had to struggle not just with the Kalashnikov but also, like the Pakistani authorities, with the culture of the Kalashnikov. A deadly illustration of this scenario occurred on the night of 22 July 2003, when the news broke that the Americans had killed Saddam Hussein's hated sons Qusai and Odai. So many AKs were fired into the air above Baghdad that it literally rained bullets: at least one GI died and scores of Iraqis were wounded by rounds that went straight up and then came down again at deadly speed. When Iraqis celebrated a wedding, a birthday or even the opening of a new village hall they fired their AKs in the air, and for the first year of the occupation US infantrymen would respond with devastating power. In September 2003, for instance, US troops responded to celebratory fire at a wedding party in Fallujah by killing a fourteen-year-old boy and wounding six adults. The policy of American front-line units was simply this: if you hear shooting and it's not from your side, fire back at it until it stops. But in Iraq you can always hear shooting. Individual American officers attempted to persuade GIs to adopt less devastating responses, but at the command level America was blind to the harm that such incidents inflicted. Indeed, the high command stepped up the scale of the response: in May 2004 air strikes against a wedding party near the Syrian border killed forty-five people. In justification, occupation officials claimed there had been Kalashnikovs in the building. This was true: a year earlier, in May 2003, Paul Bremer, the most senior American official in Iraq, gave notice that the occupation forces would allow Iraqis to maintain one AK per household for 'family defence', although other 'military-style' weapons must be handed in.

When I arrived in Iraq in January 2004 the clash between the coalition and the Iraqi resistance was quickly on the way to becoming one of the defining conflicts in the Kalashnikov's history, and if I wanted to understand the gun's continuing potency it was a conflict I had to witness. I went up in an RAF Hercules from Basra in the British occupied zone and flew high over the desert before swooping down to cross Baghdad's outlying suburbs. The pilot took the plane low over the rooftops to avoid gunfire and rockets, releasing silver chaff as he weaved to confuse heat-seeking missiles. He wasn't too concerned about AK fire. 'It should bounce off,' he said with a trademark insouciance that did little to settle my fractured nerves. He flew so low that the co-pilot was obliged to call out when he saw electricity or telephone wires so we could jump over them. Then the Hercules' alarm went off, signalling that a missile had locked on to us. For two minutes the pilot took the plane through a series of tight turns and dropped more chaff. When we landed the co-pilot said, 'Sorry about that. False alarm.' This gave me the advantage of already being scared out of my wits when I met the unit with whom I was due to be embedded.

From the massive military base around Baghdad airport I drove in a three-Humvee convoy to south-west Baghdad, which, to use the phrase of the man manning the overhead machine gun, 'is a pretty fucking tricky place'. Inside Wolf Base on the edge of the city I found the men from Alpha Company sitting around the company command room. They had recently been told they would be recalled soon, and although they had been told the same thing before and nothing had come of it they were allowing themselves to hope. 'Of course we're scared,' said a twenty-year-old from Louisiana. 'To get this close to going home and be killed—it's frightening.'

The soldier and his comrades were spearhead troops who had charged across the desert the year before. Since President Bush's infamous declaration of the end of the war from the deck of the USS *Abraham Lincoln* on 1 May 2003 they had seen their comrades killed by snipers, RPGs, roadside IEDs (improvised explosive devices, roadside charges of explosives and metal fragments that can be set off by the electrical remote control for garage doors or a TV) and mortar attacks. A week earlier two men had died and two had been critically injured when a device had exploded underneath their Humvee. An officer who had been in a convoy that had been hit the previous month told me that 'after the explosion they come out and shoot at the survivors with AKs. Not on a big convoy—they know we have the firepower to blow them away. But with a small convoy, maybe two or three Humvees, you can have problems. Three or four well-positioned men with AKs can keep you pinned down until a chopper comes. Sometimes they have a guy with an RPG waiting near by to have a shot at the chopper, but you would have to be extremely brave to do that because the choppers can clear a very large area very quickly. Either way you're out there in the road being shot at with an AK.'

Along the corridor outside the command room photographs of the company's fatalities were tacked up alongside small plastic stars and stripes; they made for a sombre walk to bed. After a restless night in a sleeping bag I joined a morning patrol through the scrubby suburbs of south Baghdad. The mission, according to the lieutenant's briefing, was to drive out to some nearby villages, dismount and walk around. Patrols like these were meant to assure the local population that US forces were in charge and to befriend village leaders. When we set off, the sergeant in my Humvee gave me a more succinct mission objective: 'Get in there and get the fuck out without being shot or blown up.'

We spent an hour driving nervously between a confusion of hamlets and suburbs, getting out occasionally so the lieutenant in charge of the patrol could talk to the local sheik or mukhtar. Inside the Humvees the men were susceptible to IEDs, but they were far more likely to be shot outside their vehicles where they were easier targets for the AKs of an enemy they couldn't see.

The soldier working the radio alongside the sergeant turned to me and said, 'If they come at you and they're shooting, just stand still. As long as they're aiming at you, you won't be hit.' Given the Kalashnikov's rate of fire, I suggested, this seemed an ill-advised tactic—they'd have to hit me eventually even if they weren't aiming at me. The sergeant started to laugh. 'Shit, no! Don't stand still, get under something or back in the Humvee as quick as you can. Don't worry—we'll be there before you.'

Instead of driving to our last village, we walked across scrubland. The Humvees were sent ahead to wait for us on the opposite side. Until now children and herds of sheep and goats had followed us, but as we approached through puddles of sewage and piles of discarded trash there was no sign of life at all. The men walked close to the walls of the houses, working their way to the home of the mukhtar in the centre of the village. The lieutenant asked him whether the water truck was coming regularly and if the village was getting enough power. These were seemingly mundane questions, but vital if the lieutenant wanted to stop the village being a willing host to gunmen. The Kalashnikov thrives on misery and much of the city still only got electricity for four hours a day—and even that often failed completely—while fresh water came from standpipes or water trucks. Ali, the eighteen-year-old Iraqi interpreter, translated the mukhtar's answers. Ali wore a ski mask to hide his identity: if the resistance discovered he worked for the Americans, he would be shot or worse. Other interpreters had been tortured to death.

Neither power nor water trucks had come to the village that week, and as the lieutenant attempted to appease the increasingly angry mukhtar the rest of the patrol spread out and took up covering positions, looking for likely sources of sniper fire. After twenty minutes we left the mukhtar and set off to rejoin the Humvees. By now I was thoroughly unnerved by the atmosphere in the village, and very keen to get back in my Humvee and leave.

We were near the edge of the village when the shots came: crack-crack-crack. I had expected the men to hit the ground, but instead they looked around to see where the firing had come from. The lieutenant did not appear to notice at all.

'That's an AK. Get against the wall,' ordered the sergeant.

I did exactly as he said, and was joined there by Ali. Although I was scared, I was surprised that no one else was taking cover.

Then the lieutenant came to life, shouting, 'Where did that come from?'

The sergeant pointed left, to where the houses merged into the next village.

'He'll be gone. Let's get back to the vehicles,' the lieutenant said flatly.

'Yes, sir,' replied the sergeant.

As we walked down to the Humvees I asked the sergeant why they hadn't gone after the gunman.

'It's not worth it—there won't be anyone there now. Single sniper attacks come in short bursts—any longer than that is too risky for the gunman. There are so many we can't go after everyone any more, and you don't call in an air strike for one sniper. We can't even be sure he was shooting at us.'

And that was that. My first time under Kalashnikov fire—an experience I now shared with hundreds of thousands of people around the world—had been a strangely deflating event: a couple of cracks and then nothing. No one hit, and no sight of either gun or gunman.

The next day I was taken to an area where AKs had been hitting Americans. Bravo company came to the base in four Humvees to collect hot food and I joined them on their return drive to the power station they defended, three kilometres north-east of Wolf Base between the River Tigris and the east-west highway that formed the base's front perimeter. The drive took us up the main north-south highway towards central Baghdad and the supposedly safe Green Zone. Before we reached the Tigris the column turned right off the highway and on to the road that led to the power station. Immediately we encountered a long queue of battered Iraqi cars waiting at a gas station that was crowded with civilians and IPs (Iraqi police). This had been the site of many attacks on the occupying forces over the previous months. A soldier explained to me why it was so dangerous, a perfect example of how the Kalashnikov adapts to its surroundings to deadly effect.

'This is the most fucked up gas station in the world. You see that queue—that's because it only sells a little bit of gas at a time. As soon as someone leaves, someone joins, so the queue never gets any smaller. And it's not just the gas for their cars—they're also buying the gas they cook with. Sometimes they get angry and the IPs go in to calm it down by firing their AKs in the air. It doesn't make things very calm, but it clears the scene. If there's a big enough crowd someone will take a shot at the police and we have to go in. Then they'll melt away in the crowd, and we can't just open up at two hundred people and hope we get the right guy with the AK.'

When someone started shooting a Kalashnikov the men in the company called it 'a situation'. The resistance had worked out that situations at the gas station provided a good opportunity to kill Americans. Two US soldiers had been hit by AK fire there. One had been stabbed in the neck, and an RPG had been fired at knee height right down the road and, miraculously, gone through a crowd of men without hitting anyone. As we approached, it became clear there was more trouble. Fire had been reported, and at least one hundred Iraqi civilians were milling chaotically around the gas pumps. Two Humvees from Wolf were already there, the men forming a defensive cordon around the central office. An Iraqi police officer wearing mirrored sunglasses was holding a rag around his hand, which had taken a ricochet from an AK fired from somewhere near by. A US chopper was manoeuvring overhead, a heavy machine gunner sweeping his barrel across the crowd below. After a brief consultation with the other patrol our lieutenant ordered us to continue on our way to the power station. Again it appeared that the men with the AKs had simply melted away.

The mood in the Humvees was now one of tense expectation. Half a kilometre along the road an ancient orange Nissan pulled out of a side alley and tucked in behind the last Humvee, keeping pace with it. This last vehicle was equipped with a top-mounted heavy machine gun, whose gunner was now aiming directly in line with the Nissan's windscreen and shaking his head slowly from side to side. But the Nissan kept on following, so the gunner started to shout: 'Get the fuck away! Get the fuck away!' He gestured wildly at the Nissan with his left hand while keeping the gun aimed at the driver's face with his right. Finally the car slowed down, pulled over and stopped.

This last stretch before the base was officially friendly territory, but over the past two months the men had been shot at regularly as they drove through. Six months previously IEDs had been placed further away from the base at the furthest limits of the patrols, which theoretically made patrols harder to support once they had been hit and also lessened the risk for the insurgents who planted them. Now the bombs were being placed much closer to the base. The houses and alleys that surrounded it on three sides were easy to disappear into and could hide thousand of insurgents, and to explode an IED successfully took only two men—one to plant the device and another to press the button when the Americans came by. A really organized assault would involve five or six men with AKs positioned around the ambush, ready to shoot down anyone who staggered out of the wreckage.

As we neared the base the drivers gunned up their engines. And in the front seats of each vehicle one man looked left and another looked right, scanning the side of the road for anything that might be an IED. They could be hidden in plastic bags, hub caps, cardboard boxes, piles of rotten vegetables, palm fronds—anything that looked like discarded trash was suspicious, and this was a country where all the trash was discarded by the side of the road.

The Humvees were ill equipped to survive an explosion. The first three vehicles were not armoured, and the men had put lengths of hardboard down the sides and inside the canvas roofs to protect themselves. Only the last Humvee, the one with a heavy machine gun, had proper armour. A

Humvee had been blown off the road late last summer and fallen on its roof in a ditch, where it had been raked with AK fire until another patrol had come round the corner and killed two insurgents. 'They were standing there shooting,' said the sergeant, 'as if they were untouchable.' Just like the men at the Al Samawah bridge, I couldn't help thinking.

We drove past the parade of small shops where a year previously, before the air force started opening fire at outbreaks of celebratory AK fire, the troops would have stopped to buy Coke, bags of crackers and cigarettes. Iraqi men stood sullenly in the doorways; some children waved, others threw stones. An Iraqi police squad car with its flashers on pulled out of our way, knowing that the Americans from the power station didn't stop or slow down for anything any more. The policemen, wearing sunglasses and smoking, raised their hands as the Humvees roared past but no one acknowledged the greeting. A kilometre from the power station, through the dirty windscreen I could see the two generating stacks that had stood blackened and useless since British Tornado fighter-bombers had hit them at the start of the war. Gunning the engine, we covered the distance in what seemed like two minutes. Lacking a flak jacket, I pressed myself as far down as I could into the Humvee as we raced through a stretch of scrubland and ramshackle houses and apartment blocks. Directly in front of the base were five tank traps to prevent potential suicide bombers, and on a two-metre-high wall of sandbags stood a heavy machine gun manned by a US soldier. Opposite him on the other side of the gate five Iraqi policemen, their AKs stacked against a wall, were gathered around a fire they had made in an oil drum.

'They don't look too worried,' the sergeant said to the driver.

The driver called over to one of the policemen, 'Heh, Ishty, is your cousin going to attack us tonight?'

'Hello, sir, no cousin tonight,' the policeman replied, smiling.

A lieutenant got down from the first Humvee and walked over to the soldier on the sandbag emplacement. 'These men are supposed to be guarding this gate with you.'

'Shit, sir, it's daylight. Nothing's going to happen,' the soldier replied.

'So you're saying the resistance only attacks the base at night so there's no point keeping guard during the day?'

The soldier considered this for a second, then said, 'Well, sir, they do only attack at night.' He pushed on the concrete block that lifted up the barrier.

Our convoy pulled past him and stopped at an inner gatehouse at the start of an avenue of palm trees that led to the two towers of the power station. At the towers we passed a ragtag group of Iraqi men who were employed on the site, wandering behind a forklift that was carrying a crate of parts. Behind the Iraqis walked two Dutch engineers, dressed in shorts and summer shirts even though it was still winter. They were the official representatives of the American company that had the contract to repair the plant. The previous week a mortar attack on the base had destroyed the hut where they kept their tools, and it was becoming apparent that the Iraqi engineers and mechanics with whom they had been supplied were not engineers and mechanics. Work on getting the plant going again was going nowhere.

Two white Land Cruisers with black windows were parked at the foot of the wrecked towers. The doors were open, and inside we saw two ex-British army soldiers who worked as security for the contractors inside. Both were cradling sub-machine guns on their laps.

Beyond them we turned left into a compound in front of a small single-storey barracks building. On the roof there was another sandbag position manned by four IPs who smiled down as the men dismounted from their Humvees. Twenty-five metres away on the other side of the compound stood four plastic toilet cubicles mounted on a concrete plinth and aligned in a row so that the doors faced away from the barracks. The sergeant explained the slightly incongruous toilets. 'Someone from the Engineer Corps decided that was the right distance for stopping the smell from the johns coming into the windows, but not so far that we couldn't get back from them safely if the base was attacked.' Evidently it was an optimistic equation, calculated before the base had come under regular mortar and AK fire; and the men didn't use the cubicles after midnight, when the resistance would open fire from the other side of the highway.

The men dismounted from the Humvees and pulled off their helmets and flak jackets. Some of them went into a huddle to pray, thanking God for getting them through another patrol without being maimed or killed. Others sat down where they were and opened cans of Coke that they fished out of a garbage can full of ice. Everyone smoked.

The driver had joked with Ishty about his cousin being in the resistance, but many of the IPs had connections with someone who knew when trouble was going to start. At night, when one company was out on patrol and the other was standing down, the IPs defended the base with a finely honed sense of self-protection. They had a habit of disappearing just before the AK rounds came clattering up the avenue or the mortars started to thud into the compound. If you went out at night and you couldn't see the IPs on the roof or down at the gatehouse it was advisable to get back in the barracks quickly because something bad was going to happen any minute. Despite this the IPs were kept on at the base, and the Americans were friendly towards them as they represented several AKs that were firing out of rather than into the compound.

I stayed with the men at the power station for two nights. On the second night I wandered down to the gate and joined a group of soldiers standing around a brazier with the IPs. Then a brief burst of AK fire sounded from down the road. The soldiers looked up.

I asked, 'Will you go out and investigate that fire?'

The sergeant shook his head. 'No. The sun's going down—they won't send us out to investigate. We don't have anyone out there at the moment. It's just Iraqis—they're either hitting IPs or taking each other out.'

Two days later I returned to Baghdad airport to hitch an RAF flight back to Basra. On the way our convoy drove past a group of IPs manning a roadblock. I noticed that many of the men had customized their AKs, mostly by removing the butt. This gives an AK an even more distinctive profile—that of a super-charged pistol rather than an assault rifle. It fits well with the Wild West approach that many Iraqis have to their guns, but renders an AK hopelessly inaccurate in combat as the barrel will kick up and away from any target at which it is levelled once automatic fire is engaged. Yet it spoke volumes about the Iraqi love affair with the Kalashnikov—even the police treated it as a flamboyant symbol of masculinity. If that was how the forces of law and order behaved, I wondered while waiting for the RAF to get me out of there, what chance did the country have? Would it ever escape the shadow of the gun? Other observers would see similar things. In April 2004 John Burns of the *New York Times* encountered a disparate group of militiamen in Fallujah: 'Some of the militiamen were in their fifties and sixties, but most were young, some no more than twelve or thirteen. Weapons training among them appeared virtually nonexistent; Kalashnikovs with loaded magazines and safety catches off were nonchalantly waved in the air.'

In the spring of 2004 I flew to Izhevsk and met General Kalashnikov. He was rather taken by the fact that I had been shot at by AK47s. Not because of any bravery on my behalf—and sadly there had been little—but by my perceived dedication to the subject in hand. 'You must be serious about my gun,' he suggested with approval. I was, having seen the AK47 exert a pull on the Iraqi conflict that seemed out of proportion to its capabilities. After all, it was just a gun that was easily available to anyone in the Middle East, yet it was mounting a serious opposition to the overwhelming force of the American killing machines arrayed against it in Iraq.

Back in its earliest days, as the AK47 went into full production in 1948, the Berlin Airlift had sounded the Cold War's opening salvo and the threat of conflict with the United States had informed the general's career from that point until the fall of communism. Although he become friendly with Eugene Stoner, inventor of the M16, after the collapse of the Soviet Union (he had visited him on several occasions in the USA) the fact remained that Kalashnikov had spent the bulk of his professional life designing weapons to kill Americans. He was clearly almost childishly curious about the Americans' opinion of the AK's performance in Iraq.

'Tell me,' he asked, 'what do the American troops in Iraq say about my gun?'

'They are amazed by its ability to resist the sand and dust. They have trouble with their rifles—they misfire occasionally because of the conditions. But they have captured resistance AKs which clearly haven't been cleaned properly for days but were still successfully fired.'

He smiled at that. 'Life has come full circle, then. The M16 has failed to match the AK47 before.'

As it had in Vietnam, Kalashnikov's weapon was showing itself it to be better than the M16. American troops were again complaining that their own automatic weapons were not performing well. In Iraq it wasn't heat and damp but sand and fine dust that were causing their weapons to jam, and in order to keep them operational spare time became rifle-cleaning time.

And the general was obviously happy about the performance of his gun. 'I made it to work in all climatic conditions,' he boasted with clear pride in his voice.

On my return to Britain I discovered that newspaper and television reports were increasingly featuring attacks on the occupying forces in Iraq. Despite the positive 'situation reports' of their senior officers and the Pentagon from May 2003 onwards, America had created in Iraq the conditions for the full-scale uprising that began in the spring of 2004. Bringing order to the Iraqi population and restoring the basic infrastructure slipped further down the agenda as attacks steadily increased. GIs were now unwilling to leave their bases to go on patrols that regularly featured the Iraqi resistance double-whammy of an IED explosion on the roadside followed by intense AK fire directed at troops trying to rescue their comrades from stricken vehicles. I had seen the beginning of this reluctance with the US Airborne, but they had gone home now and I wondered how other elements in the US army were handling a large-scale Kalashnikov insurrection. A month after John Burns had watched militiamen holding their AKs aloft I returned to Iraq.

In the half-year that I had been away the US army had withdrawn into its heavily fortified bases where it hunkered down and waited to be pulled out. For ordinary American infantrymen planned, confrontational fighting with the enemy was becoming the exception, broken only by sporadic and fearsome occasions such as the November 2004 assault on Fallujah, when they operated behind tanks and fighter-bombers in large-scale assaults on regional centres of militancy. Things had clearly taken a turn for the worse—by now the Sunni tactic of beheading Western hostages was in full swing—but I was as hooked on the sound of a Kalashnikov as any other reporter in a war zone and wanted to see for myself what effect the men with roadside bombs and Kalashnikovs were having on the coalition.

For my second trip I was attached to the 1st Armored Division. After another nerve-shaking flight and three days waiting in intense heat at the Baghdad airport base I was sent to Camp War Eagle on the edge of Sadr City. Sadr is a teeming slum of 2 million mainly Shiite inhabitants to the immediate north-east of Baghdad and, in 2004, the home turf of the militant cleric Muqtada al-Sadr's al-Mahdi army. An ex-Iraq army base, which Saddam had used, as the Americans were doing now, to keep a close watch on this traditionally rebellious settlement, War Eagle was surrounded by a two-metre-high brick and cement wall, razor wire and sandbags. A four-storey flat-roofed building which the Americans used as their operational command centre stood in the centre and dominated the compound. Alongside the southern wall, directly facing Sadr City, was a complex of three-storey barracks which, lying nearest to the resistance mortar teams as it did, tended to be missed by incoming shells that arced over the wall and landed deeper inside the camp, but was susceptible to AK fire if any resistance fighter was brave or foolhardy enough to come close. Around the command centre a dozen Bradley fighting vehicles—a cross between an armoured car and a light tank—were drawn up in two rows of six, and on the west side of the compound a pair of helicopter gunships rested on their take-off strip.

The several hundred men in War Eagle were supposed to keep Sadr in check, but in some ways they were under siege themselves. Most nights they were mortared and fired upon by al-Sadr's men, and by day they took their Humvee patrols deep into Sadr's sewage-soaked streets where each lamp-post and wall appeared to be plastered with posters of al-Mahdi's leader. The civilians that gathered around these patrols did so with that strange Iraqi mixture of sullenness and mockery that left American troops on permanent edge. It was very hard to judge the mood of these crowds, so the troops' policy was to presume there was always an AK trained on the vulnerable patch of artery, flesh and cartilage between the top of their flak jackets and their chinstraps where a round would cause devastating damage.

Sitting in an open-top Humvee deep in Sadr City I felt even more vulnerable. Al-Sadr would not allow an IED to be detonated in streets packed with his supporters, but the threat of AK fire was ever-present. In the cramped and narrow lanes, where faces loomed up and hands grabbed at the Humvees despite the soldiers' shouted orders to keep away, the Kalashnikovs worked as an invisible yet all too real deterrent. I couldn't see them, but I knew they were there.

On my first night at War Eagle I went up on the roof of the four-storey central building and joined two snipers equipped with high-powered rifles and night vision telescopes. We listened to the distinctive pop-pop-pop of AKs and watched red tracer fire split the sky as men in Sadr fired their AKs into the air. It was mesmerizing and beautiful. Half hypnotized by the sound and light show that the al-Mahdi men were putting on in the black sky above the slums, it took me a while to connect it with real men and guns.

'What are they doing that for?' I asked.

'Partly to spoil our concentration. You sit here and look up at it, and then you're taken by surprise when the mortars land. They're also saying, "Look how many AKs and how much ammunition we got!"'

'They want choppers to come so they can have a shot with an RPG,' added the other sniper. 'But we haven't lost a chopper over there yet, and when we direct fire down on to the rooftops they soon stop firing.'

It seemed as if the day belonged to the Americans and their nervous Humvee patrols, and the night to the al-Mahdi army and its AKs. But, as I would shortly find out, it was during the hours of darkness that the Americans did most of their killing, as the Iraqis were still largely dismissive of the capabilities of night vision. I looked through the first sniper's night finder; it was focused on the top of a wall about 400 metres away.

'Someone puts their head over that,' said the sniper, 'and they lose it.'

No heads came over the wall that night, but twenty-four hours later I again found myself watching the AK tracer in the sky. On this occasion I was walking from the barracks to the command centre, where an operational meeting had been called for eleven o'clock. 'Something,' said the soldier who was accompanying me across the compound, 'is going to happen tonight.'

And it did. I had not heard anything, but seconds after he had spoken the soldier shouted, 'Get down!', and pushed me towards a low wall. The first mortar shell landed in the middle of the compound, hitting the ground with a loud percussive report and sending shards of red-hot metal shooting across the ground at ankle height. It was thirty metres away but I didn't move and neither did the soldier, who knew that mortar attacks came in groups of two or three shots and that if the Iraqis were running two mortar crews off the rooftops we would have a chance to get back inside in the gap between the last shot from the first mortar and the first shot from the next. As the second shot went off the first mortar crew would change their position, playing cat and mouse with the helicopter crews and observation drones that scouted the sky above them. Any more than three shots and the crews risked being spotted by the choppers and coming under cannon fire. Another mortar fell in the compound, this time on the far side away from the barracks.

The third bomb had barely landed when the soldier sprang up and we ran to the operational centre. Inside, the place was alive with shouting men. The mortar attack would be over in a few more minutes, but orders for a chopper to fly over Sadr had already gone out and the captain was calling for quiet amongst the assembled officers and NCOs. It quickly became apparent that we were also going out on the ground, and in force. At their request I have changed the names of key personnel, but the events that unfolded that night were happening to similar men across the country and, in the case of the Kalashnikov gunmen we went out to fight, all over the world.

The captain who addressed the meeting wasn't happy. No one had been killed, but the base had been attacked and he appeared to be taking it personally. 'The local population think it's okay to shoot at us and mortar us. That's fine—let them think like that. But I want to go out there tonight and show them what *we* can do.' The captain pointed to a plan of Sadr City pinned to the wall at one end of the conference room. 'We're going to take two columns of four Bradleys into Sadr. Column One is going to go around to the east and drive to the central point here.' He picked out an area of relatively open ground where the main roads from north to south and east to west bisected each other in the centre of Sadr. 'I want this first column to make plenty of noise when it gets there. I want the whole of Sadr to know you are there.' He nodded at the lieutenant, who would be in the first Bradley, as he said this.

'You just want us to sit there and let them shoot at us, sir?'

'Exactly, Lieutenant. And when they do, there will be a Bradley behind them that will take them out.'

This wasn't the risky endeavour that at first I took it to be. A Bradley is protected by reactive armour that explodes on contact with any incoming missile or shell and pushes the force of the impact away from the vehicle. There is absolutely no prospect of AK fire damaging, let alone entering, a sealed and combat-ready Bradley. An assailant's only hope of success is that the hatch has been left open or that he will come across a Bradley with its tailgate down, in which case the inside of the vehicle would become an inescapable killing chamber. But such was the Kalashnikov's status among Iraqi males that the resistance would shoot at the most unlikely targets. Whether they thought they could actually stop an armoured car, tank or even helicopter with an AK only they knew, but the Americans were well aware that al-Mahdi gunmen were willing to come out and shoot at almost anything in the dark even if the chances of success were apparently nil.

The captain turned to Hanson, the sergeant who would lead the second column. 'You head down from the north and park up here. Turn off your engines and just sit there. I figure the noise from our Humvees will cover your noise. We'll be the main event in town. I don't think they will be looking for a Bradley at the back, and anyway it will be black out there—the power's down again tonight. If they don't hear you they won't look for you, and if they don't look for you they won't see you. We'll wait till they come out to fire at us and then, when you get a clear target, let them have it with the chain gun.'

The M242 25mm 'Bushmaster' chain gun mounted on a Bradley (the vehicles are also equipped with an M240 machine gun) can fire two hundred 25mm explosive shells per minute and will destroy anything not made of metal that gets in its way.

'If they wander round the alleys with AKs,' the captain continued, 'then we can kill them in the alleys. But the usual rules—try and get a definite ID on a weapon before you fire.'

I got the distinct impression that this operational caveat was made because I was there rather than out of any deeply held conviction about avoiding civilian casualties. The only 'usual rule' in Sadr City was: kill them before they kill you.

But would someone try to kill me? As yet I didn't know if I would be going along for the ride or not. The men at War Eagle had no obligation to take me on offensive operations, and I thought they might limit my participation to day patrols rather than take an inexperienced, possibly unsympathetic extra body on a search-and-destroy mission. But being caught out in the open during the mortar attack had temporarily gifted me a certain amount of fellow feeling from the men and as we left the command room Hanson approached me.

'Hey, you okay now?'

'Yes, I'm fine.'

'Great. You coming with us?'

I didn't need to be asked twice.

As we gathered at Hanson's Bradley the crew showed me battle scars on the armour, pointing out the difference between hits from AK rounds and those from RPGs. Both seemed to have negligible effect, though in places metal showed through the sand-coloured paintwork. We left the base at 10.30, an hour before the al-Mahdi mortar teams would be in place in northern Sadr City; nonetheless it was presumed that we were being observed, and as we left another chopper took off to clear any watching gunmen from the rooftops.

Inside the Bradley I was alone in the rear compartment, where I could watch a screen showing the same images as would be seen by the gunner up above in the turret and the driver up front in the cab. In ten minutes the back of the vehicle had filled with sand and the smell of the other men's cigarette smoke, and was badly overheated. When we turned out on to the highway that ran along the side of Sadr City the driver tried to avoid the potholes and ruts, but it was nearly impossible in the dark and I was subjected to violent shaking and jolting. After ten minutes the column split as planned: four Humvees went around to the east for a long loop around the city's outskirts, while my column entered Sadr and struck southwards. We were scheduled to meet again an hour later in the centre of the city.

Over the radio the two columns checked each other's position occasionally, while our driver and gunner exchanged small talk over the Bradley's intercom. Hanson kept quiet, speaking only to reply to requests for his progress from the other column. The gunner, who was traversing his Bushmaster from left to right, spotted gunmen flitting between buildings. Another gunner in the second column saw them as well, and requests for permission to shoot started to fill up the airwaves. The captain came over on the radio, ordering the men in the second column to hold fire.

'Wait until we are in position. I don't want them hiding yet. Do not open fire.'

When he was not lurching into potholes or swerving over the central reservation the driver was getting very precise about just what he was going to do with a certain girl when he got back to Minnesota. And how much beer he would drink before he did it to her.

It was a strange way to go to war, and I wondered what General Kalashnikov would think of such subterfuge and effort to track down and then destroy the men who carried his gun. He was a natural hunter, a man who spent as much time as he could tracking elk so that his housekeeper could make him soup. But had he ever imagined that other men would go hunting for his invention or that the tactics of a superpower—the only superpower since his beloved Soviet Union had faded away—would be concentrated on smashing the men who carried his gun?

The gunner wasn't interested in sex, or if he was he didn't want to talk about it. By now he was fired up for combat and was showing off, for my sake maybe, about how many resistance fighters he had killed. 'Must be forty now. As soon as I see that AK shape I know I got them—that's my green light to fire. I could recognize that silhouette anywhere—that's all I need, and then I take them. When these shells hit them there's no more resistance, no more AKs, no more nothing. Just shit and smoke. This chain gun could knock down their fucking houses.'

As the gunner laughed at his own words the driver joined in. I realized that the crew must perform a version of this ceremony every time they went out to war in their formidable killing machine. There was no sane way of deploying a Bradley against human beings, so perhaps they needed to make themselves temporarily mad before taking on Sadr City's shadowy Kalashnikov gunmen. Or perhaps, like me, they were scared.

'What about that guy you missed last week?' asked the driver.

'I never miss, man. Just point me at something and I'll blow it apart.'

'Come on—you know you fucking missed a guy with an AK and a guy with an RPG right next to him.'

'I didn't miss them,' said the gunner, who looked no older than nineteen, 'I chose to let him live.'

The gunner and driver disintegrated with laughter, and the Bradley veered to the left and into a pothole. I vomited quietly and quickly in the back, then washed the sick to the very rear of the vehicle with two cans of Coca-Cola I had brought along to keep me awake.

'Hey, Michael, you all right back there?' asked the driver, but he was laughing too much to find out.

Eventually the Bradley swung right, drove along a track for 200 metres and came to a halt. We waited, saying nothing at all until five minutes later the radio came alive again and confirmed that the other column was in position approximately 300 metres south of us, although we could not see them from where we were parked. I fixed my eyes on the screen as the gunner aimed his sights directly down a lane to our right that ran parallel to the other column's position. It took me a moment to adjust my vision to the strange world of green and white shapes produced by the night vision camera. From outside the Bradley I could hear the roar of the other column driving in low gear, trying to tempt the gunmen out. Inside, the crew settled down to wait.

They didn't have to wait for long. After seven minutes by my watch the gunner spoke.

'Here we go—left-hand side halfway up the lane on the right side.'

The lane sloped upwards and away from our position, and there were cars parked on both sides. I searched in vain for a figure as I listened to the crew's increasingly excited conversation.

Hanson could see him, though: 'About fifty metres up. Right behind the car on the right-hand side on the second corner. You got it?'

The gunner replied, 'Yeah, yeah, there's something there.' Suddenly I saw it. Fifty metres away a head had emerged from a doorway, shining ghostly and white against the dull green background.

For my benefit the driver whispered over the intercom, 'The Iraqis don't do night vision—they don't realize they can be seen.'

The driver was about to continue, but the sound of AK fire stopped him short. A voice came over the radio, high-pitched and jerky.

'What have you got there? We're under fire here.'

I could hear the other Bradleys returning fire in short punching bursts.

'We got something, sir, but it isn't the guys who are firing at you.'

I returned to the screen. The first head had grown into a pair of shoulders, and next to them was the outline of an AK's double-ended barrel and oversized sight-finder.

'Oh, yeah, now we've got one!' The driver's voice was a mixture of venom and joy. 'Come on, motherfucker, come on out. We're going to warm you up. Out you come.'

The man went back in, then came out again with another man who also carried an AK. They both looked up and then down the alley. The second man, perhaps a commander, appeared to be more certain of himself and walked between the parked cars and out into the middle of the alley. He looked down in the direction of the Bradley. He couldn't possibly see it in the darkness, but he kept looking straight ahead at the place where we were parked as if he was aware that there was something down there that was defeating his senses. On the screen he registered as the unmistakeable figure of a man carrying a Kalashnikov.

'Right, I got him.'

'Don't fire!' commanded Hanson. 'Wait till I say, "Fire." Understand?'

The gunfire had abated now and a voice came back on the radio. 'They've stopped firing, but we don't know if we've hit anything. Have you got contact?'

Hanson responded. 'Yeah, we've got two. We can open fire now, but we think there may be another one. They're kind of coming out, kind of staying in. Can you guys make some noise? I want to get this third guy out of the house.'

There was a muffled order on the radio, and the heavy machine gun started up again. I could hear it over the radio and from outside the Bradley. The man in the alley turned away from our position and looked across the alley towards the noise, peering into the dark and not realizing that he was the hunted rather than the hunter.

'Yeah, he heard that. I've got him now. I'm just waiting for the other guy.'

The first man looked up and down the alley, then turned back towards the doorway to say something, at which point a third man emerged from the doorway. He was carrying an AK as well and, like the other two, looked directly at the Bradley without seeing it. Then all three turned away towards the noise from the other column. Finally a fourth head came out, that of a man who appeared to be disagreeing with the first man, who motioned him back indoors with his AK.

The gunner talked them through. 'Yes, come on, step outside. Come on, come on.'

Hanson's voice, high-pitched and insistent, came over the intercom. 'Have we got a shot? Have we got a shot?'

Unlike Hanson, the gunner had become calmer as he approached the moment when he would open fire. 'Sir, I've got three shots but I can't confirm on the fourth. I can't see if he's armed.'

'He shouldn't be talking to men with Kalashnikovs. Have you got a shot yet?'

'Just on the first three, sir. I can't get the fourth.'

'Go ahead, fire, and fire!'

The Bradley shook with the force of the outgoing fire, and the cramped space where I had tried to make myself comfortable filled with dust and the stench of cordite.

The driver was yelling. 'Go on, kill the motherfuckers!'

The gunner was now laughing loudly as he sent scores of high-explosive cannon shells pouring into the alleyway in front of him.

The fourth figure had got back inside the door, but the other three men carrying Kalashnikovs were caught in a shower of high-velocity metal and flame. I struggled to understand the images I was watching. The system had a tendency to turn any pale material into bright white, and amidst the flickering green and white images on the screen the first man looked as if he was wearing a white shirt. Then I saw the wound that ended the man's life, and the rest of the image suddenly fell into place. A shot entered his body just above the chest on his left-hand side. Immediately the night vision screen registered a black hole in the white shirt, but the man seemed to take a second or two to register the fact himself. He was still standing, even though the exit wound must have blown most of his lungs, heart and spine out of the other side of his body. It was clear he had been killed immediately, and mystifying that he could remain upright for three or four seconds after receiving such a massive impact. The other men were splattered with his blood and still unaware in the dark of where the fire was coming from. As they turned to run down the alley the second man was lifted from his feet by a shot. The third man continued to run down the alley towards the Bradley, firing his AK from the waist as the chain gun continued to fire and the street exploded and splintered around him until a round hit him fully in the stomach and hurled him down.

The gunner was yelling, 'Got him! Got him! I fucking got him!'

Over the intercom Hanson was talking to the captain. 'Three down. We got three down. Three kills here.'

We got back to the base at two o'clock. The captain smashed his palms against the side of the Bradleys and the Humvees, then slapped the backs of the men getting out. It had been a good mission. Apart from the three gunmen that Hanson's Bradley had accounted for the first column was claiming two kills—although who could tell how many non-combatants had been killed or injured when the Bradley's cannon shells had blasted through the flimsy walls of Sadr City's lanes and alleyways. So, at considerable expense to the American taxpayer, there were now five fewer fighters in Sadr City. But even as our column turned round and headed back to Camp War Eagle, fresh hands were reaching out to pick up the fallen guns.

During that long Sadr City night I'd listened uncomfortably to the ping-ping-ping that an AK round makes when it hits a steel door, but I had never been in real danger. The Bradley I drove in had been near impregnable. Only fools would attack it with AK47s, yet as I watched, the al-Mahdi army fighters had come out to attempt it with almost transcendent arrogance. Across Iraq the resistance in its many forms, the militias and even the police force didn't just fire their AKs but wielded them in the air, as if the very iconic nature of the semi-automatic rifle had entered into the men themselves. The Americans had killed five, just as they had killed as many as twenty fighters on other nights, but as the young gunner told me when we got back to War Eagle and he pulled himself wearily out of his hatch, 'Doesn't seem to matter how many I kill—

they keep on coming back, night after night, firing AKs at us.'

I had seen the AK become more than a gun. In Iraq, as in Vietnam, the AK47 operates as a symbol of resistance to the United States, although in Iraq the symbolism of the AK sometimes seems to be of superior importance to its mechanical abilities. The Viet Cong did not knowingly raise up their AK47s as a signifier of their fight, but Iraqi resistance fighters do so regularly. America's occupation has become one of the most effective marketing campaigns that the Kalashnikov has ever benefited from. As long as American forces stay, be it for five or ten years, each day enhances the gun's image, each Bradley mission into the heart of Sadr City confirms its potency and the threat it poses to those who wield power in the world. In Iraq the Kalashnikov has finally become, to the long-lasting detriment of the country and misery of its inhabitants, the people's gun.

In the summer of 2004, Vladimir Putin sent George W. Bush a bottle of Russian vodka. The bottle was made of crystal and shaped like a Kalashnikov assault rifle—an unusual gift for a teetotal president who had avoided the military draft for Vietnam and consequently never heard an AK fired in anger. Perhaps the gift was an acknowledgement that US troops, like those of Russia, were being shot at with AKs every day. In every conflict zone in which Russia and America were engaged, their troops were encountering the AK47. In putting the vodka bottle in the hands of the US president, Putin was both recognizing the AK's might and rule and asking Russia to be allowed to profit from its offspring's worldwide success. Putin was reminding Bush where the Kalashnikov came from, and in doing so he was admitting where the Kalashnikov had gone. The motherland didn't matter any more; it was America where the AK was doing its business.

The US government had just ordered forty thousand brand-new AKs for the new Iraqi police force that was to be deployed in the few urban areas that American military planners felt might be open to Iraqi control. The deployment was supposed to leave US forces free to concentrate on the many other places, such as Fallujah and much of Baghdad, where there was a Kalashnikov-and-roadside-bomb uprising against the American occupation. Although the new Iraqi police force existed more as an ambition than a reality the USA was desperate to demonstrate back home that it was moving towards disengagement from what had become a disastrous occupation. The AKs were intended as public proof of the disengagement. Once more the Kalashnikov was acting as weapon and signifier in equal measure.

But the US government had not ordered its weapons from the Izhmash in Izhevsk; it had gone instead to Arsenal, the former Bulgarian state arms manufacturer, and ordered AK74s, a direct copy of the Soviet 1974 update of the AKM. This was the AK model that the left-wing Sandinistas had used against the Contras, the US right-wing client army, in the Nicaraguan civil war of the late 1970s, and it had also armed the Syrian army, which constituted a direct threat to Israel, America's main ally in the Middle East.

The US government did not comment on these paradoxes. Nor did it acknowledge that the purchase was a direct admission of the hegemony of the AK in the Middle East and simultaneously a demonstration of its own weakness in Iraq. Washington was more interested in saving money than face: as I knew Izhmash AKs cost US $500 and Bulgarian ones US $100.

In 2004 the Izhevsk plants were producing only ten to fifteen thousand rifles year. If the contract had gone to Izhmash it could have returned Izhevsk's run-down factories and overgrown streets to something like the glory days they had known thirty years before. The Russian export company, Rosobonexport, bitterly denounced the former vassal state for cashing in on what was, in their eyes, still Russian technology. But they were finding out to their cost that the now capitalist ex-satellites were not inclined to pay for using patents that their former communist allies had given away in the mid-1960s. The artfully crafted gift from Putin to Bush, then, was a reminder, a glittering yet succinct way of saying that the Kalashnikov is our gun, as Russian as vodka.

But it wasn't. Although still torturing its motherland in Chechnya and beyond, the gun that Mikhail Kalashnikov had described as a Golem, the animated imp of Yiddish legend, had shifted shape again. On the streets and television screens of America the AK would combine the imagery and associations of its previous incarnations into one overwhelmingly powerful cultural package. The process of its metamorphosis into a super-brand had begun partly in response to the defeat in Vietnam, a war in which the Kalashnikov triumphed over both the American GI and his much-vaunted M16 assault rifle.

Across America Republican voting right-wing gun club members saw the AK as a totem of the enemy but simultaneously as a triumph of simple technology—the ultimate soldier's gun. It was this America, an America whose robustly right-wing political world view would come to power with Ronald Reagan in 1981, that had reeled after the ignominy of defeat in south-east Asia. But it decided that if the Viet Cong could not be defeated then American culture would defeat its dominant symbol. That victory would come, but it would be pyrrhic. Inviting the AK into your country is akin to volunteering to be injected with a virus without knowing if it will give you a cold or kill you.

In 1982 Ronald Reagan, who as governor of California had fought hard against the anti-Vietnam war movement, began the process of reimposing American military force on the world. Stung into action by the United Kingdom's successful, if costly, retaking of the Falkland Islands from Argentina that year, Reagan sent the American 7th Fleet to Lebanon and, in league with France and Italy, attempted to impose a Pax Americana on the capital, Beirut, a city in which civil war and foreign invasion had combined to create a text book Kalashnikov conflict.

Because the USA was intimately connected with Israel, one of the key participants in the Lebanese conflict, and certainly the most powerful, it was impossible for the AK-toting militiamen (Shiite, Sunni, Christian, Druze and those Palestinians who had not left with the PLO evacuation in September 1982) to see the US presence as impartial. US marines regularly came under AK and RPG fire but it was a suicide bomb, a form of attack that is almost impossible to prevent, that brought an end to the American attempt to reassert military power. In October 1983, 241 American servicemen were killed when the Marines' headquarters at Beirut international airport were car-bombed.

As other servicemen rushed to help their comrades Muslim

militiamen sniped at them with AKs from nearby houses, establishing a suicide-bomb-and-Kalashnikov partnership that continues to this day in the Middle East. In America television audiences saw the terrible carnage and destruction of the bomb-site and the footage of triumphant militiamen brandishing their AKs in the air.

The attack was immediately attributed to Hezbollah, the radical Shiite group whose flag sports an AK logo above the words 'Party of God'. Aware of the US 7th fleet aircraft carriers which were streaming off the coast of Lebanon at the time, Hezbollah quickly denied the charge, enabling several smaller Shiite groups to claim responsibility. Whichever group was responsible, the bomb smashed American morale and made domestic calls to withdraw from a war with few potential benefits irresistible. Humiliated, and still being sniped at by AKs, in February 1984 the Marines pulled out of Beirut.

The only war which the US had won outright since 1945, and the only victory against an enemy armed with Kalashnikovs, had been the invasion of the Caribbean island of Grenada by seven thousand US troops. Those same troops posed for photographs next to captured boxes of AKs, as if the very presence of the guns was enough to prove that Maurice Bishop's elected government was an expansionist communist threat to the whole region rather than being a mildly bossy experiment in tropical island socialism.

Hand in hand with the US military, Hollywood was the vehicle for the Kalashnikov's rise in America's cultural consciousness. At first this manifested itself as a tentative coming to terms with the fact that America had been defeated, and at the same time established an excuse for that defeat. The North Vietnamese and Viet Cong troops were represented as unreal cartoon figures characterized by their propensity to cackle. They were shown as inhuman in contrast to American soldiers, who were weakened by their humanity—even though the USA had fought the war in an utterly ruthless manner. If the USSR had carpet-bombed a Third World country and dropped chemical agents on its population the US government would have denounced its leaders as war criminals—

nonetheless these measures were not enough to beat a determined and ideologically charged people's army carrying Kalashnikovs. The logic remained and was reinforced: defeat in Vietnam was not America's fault; its soldiers had been fighting an enemy that was evil.

In 1979 Michael Cimino's film *The Deer Hunter* crystallized in a single famous, harrowing scene this interpretation of America's tortuous experience in Vietnam. A group of captured GIs are forced by their Vietnamese captors to play Russian roulette with a pistol. The Vietnamese, armed with Chinese model 56s, stand around and laugh, placing bets on who will blow his head off first. Despite an intense performance from Robert De Niro as Michael, the prisoner whose sheer force of will drives the ensuing slaughter of the Vietnamese guards and escape of the GIs, the AK is the real star of the scene. At the dénouement of the 'game' De Niro's character takes the handgun they have given him to play roulette with and, after persuading his captors to put more bullets in it, turns the gun on him and shoots. Grabbing the guard's AK, he then kills the other guards. When Michael takes the AK in his hand he becomes a redeemed man, a warrior who can be just as merciless as the enemy yet not lose his humanity. A better metaphor for domestic America's growing love affair with the AK would be hard to find. Immediately after De Niro's character kills the Vietnamese guards there is a pause before the Americans escape. It allows us to consider both the bravery demonstrated in what has just happened and the enormity of what the Americans have been through. More pertinently for America's future the camera dwells on the Vietnamese corpses, and we see just what an AK47 can do to a room full of people whom you don't like.

Although liberal in its intention, *The Deer Hunter* presents a portrait of the Vietnamese as devils with AKs. In the 1980s racist portrayals of the Vietnamese and, indeed, of foreign communists in general became even more pronounced in American films. Openly aggressive and completely impervious to historical reality, Hollywood invented an unlikely scenario in which the Vietnam War had not been lost but was still being fought by one man. That one man was Rambo, as played by Sylvester Stallone, in a series of films that reinvent America's defeat as a victory. The communists—Viet Cong, North Vietnamese and Soviet advisers—were played as pantomime villains. They were invariably armed with Kalashnikovs. And so was Rambo.

In *Rambo: First Blood Part II* (1985), a film that represents the height of the genre, Rambo is sent to rescue American prisoners of war from North Vietnamese torture camps and is captured himself. Like Michael in *The Deer Hunter* Rambo turns his captors' AK against them but, in what were increasingly confident and literally muscular times, he goes one better then De Niro's character by directing the NVA soldier's AK at America's communist enemy whilst the NVA soldier is still holding it. Rambo then instigates a mini-orgy of violence and kills three more NVA with their own weapon before, in an almost erotically violent crescendo, he takes the AK and shoots blind over his shoulder, destroying the NVA soldier's head. In that moment the art of shooting an AK is given an all-American, flippantly cool styling: John Wayne meets the Kalashnikov.

Given Rambo's unlikely technique, accuracy was clearly not a key concern in films that were essentially mythic in intent. At one point in *First Blood Part II* Rambo drops his AK, and a close-up shot shows that the fire selector is in the safety position even though Rambo has been shooting hundreds of rounds from it (something he is apparently able to do without changing magazines). After twenty years such mistakes and the poverty of the script and acting make the Rambo films appear both jingoistic and laughable, but in attempting to reclaim victory for the USA they had the very serious effect of making the AK cool for a generation of young Americans. *First Blood Part II* marks the cultural turning point for the AK: gun clubs had established the product's performance credentials and introduced thousands of rifles to the country, Rambo provided an advertising campaign that was perfect for a newly emerging market.

Stallone delivered the AK to American culture, and in the mid-1980s American culture was world culture. Rambo became the pin-up hero of the decade, a right-wing, monosyllabic Che Guevara, and the AK joined soft rock and Coca-Cola in the list of internationally successful products that were sought for what they represented as much as for what they actually were or did. Posters appeared all over the world (especially, it is worth noting, in the Arab world) depicting the muscle-bound and bandana-clad Stallone holding what had previously been the weapon that represented the enemy of all that Ronald Reagan's America stood for. As a result the AK achieved a level of publicity and PR saturation far beyond anything it had achieved in its Soviet or freedom-fighting incarnations. This was more than the cover of *Time* magazine; it was world domination.

American gun clubs that were specifically committed to the use of the AK or its derivatives had been in existence since the 1970s. These clubs allowed overweight suburbanites to drive out to the shooting range, sink a few beers and wield what had been the weapon of the enemy and was now, in the hands of Rambo, refashioning the world as a place where America was triumphant. US armaments companies began to make their own AKs, re-engineering the Kalashnikov as an American product. As early as 1976 Bingham Ltd. of Norcross, Georgia was producing an AK that had been reconfigured to fire a .22 round and marketed as a sporting gun. In Santa Ana, California, Mitchell Arms imported and distributed automatic weapons, and from 1985 to 1994 they manufactured two different .22 AK clones. Bingham's AKs had stocks of beech and walnut to emphasize their woodsman credentials, but for all the marketing and luxury finishes these were still semi-automatic rifles that were more suited to the battlefield than to the sporting club.

In the late 1990s gun club Internet sites offered AKs for sale alongside claims for their unique combat capabilities. They celebrated the fall of communism but also expressed admiration for its martial values: the Red Army had 'rocked' and Kursk had been an 'awesome' tank battle. The unemployed citizens of Izhevsk were surprised to see small parties of American gun enthusiasts making a pilgrimage to their run-down city. Rambo, the death of communism and the possession of the AK...it looked as though the world's most powerful country had finally tamed the world's most notorious weapon.

Gradually America became willing to impose itself physically on the world, the fear of body bags mitigated by the immense technological superiority that US forces could take to the battlefield. Stealth bombers, a new generation of attack helicopters, the latest assault rifles and Abrams tanks: what could a few Third World peasants with Kalashnikovs do against such power? Within a few short years the lessons of Vietnam were already being forgotten. But the successful liberation of Kuwait in 1991 appeared to prove that the wheel had turned. The Iraqi army that the USA chased out of that country was armed almost entirely with AKs and could offer no defence against American military technology.

Even fresh international victories for the AK against the USA were absorbed by American culture and turned to its own marketing advantage, as in the 2001 film *Black Hawk Down* which graphically portrayed the effect of AK bullets on American bodies. The incident that inspired the book on which the film was based, a mission to arrest two militia chiefs in the Somalian capital, Mogadishu, on 3 October 1993, had resulted in the death of eighteen US combatants. American forces were in Somalia not as imperialist warmongers but as peace-keepers attempting to stabilize a country that was, like nearby Sudan where Emmanuel Jal was struggling to hold his rifle upright, blighted by hundreds of thousands of Kalashnikovs. In terms of international politics this was hearts-and-minds stuff, an attempt by the Clinton administration to establish the Americans as the good guys. The film, directed by Ridley Scott, made clear that the AK shows no respect for hearts or minds. The hundreds of AKs that can be seen in action in the film reflect in their own way the sheer number of Somalis involved in the original incident (a thousand of them were killed) and, like the Vietnam movies, Scott's film makes no serious effort to humanize the enemy but concentrates on their AKs and RPGs. The Somalis are portrayed as mad rather than evil; their desire to fight the Americans is seen as frenzied and illogical, yet the film cannot help but admire their refusal to bow down to what seems to be the immense technological superiority of the Americans' Black Hawk helicopters and heavy machine guns. Like the US military, the director is dependent on the flash and bang of high-tech special effects, but *Black Hawk Down* leaves the viewer in no doubt that the AK was the best weapon in Somalia. This much America was willing to admit; but some names that were much closer to home were omitted from the Kalashnikov world tour itinerary t-shirts. Names like Stockton, Waco and New Orleans.

As the AK became culturally predominant in the USA it leaked out of the shooting clubs and into the gun shops. Culturally it spread like ink through blotting paper from film to music, books and video. The AK had found world fame with the coming of television news reporting in the 1960s; now it hitched itself to the advent of computer entertainment. Games such as Doom and Counterstrike, and computer 'war' game culture, dislodged the Kalashnikov's meaning from its actual mechanics. Middle-class American youth took to wielding AKs voraciously in consequence-free battles across the Internet. In the privacy of their bedrooms teenagers saw only the 'cool' aspect of the AK brand. To such young men intent on inflicting carnage, the Kalashnikov provided a very specific cultural lodestar: at the most basic and deathly level, holding a Kalashnikov said, 'I am a rebel', and the Kalashnikov become the weapon of choice for a succession of angry and unhinged Americans.

In its definition of the term 'Columbine' the online Urban Dictionary gives the following example: 'The constant bullying of the preppies and jocks has caused him to pick up his AK-47 and go Columbine on everyone.' The irony was—and as we have seen, there is invariably irony with the AK—that Dylan Klebold and Eric Harris didn't use an AK. When the killers walked into Columbine High School, Colorado on 20 April 1991 they were carrying a fearsome armoury of automatic weapons, handguns and explosive devices, but no Kalashnikovs. It didn't matter; by that date the AK had become so embedded in the nation's popular culture that it was no longer important if it was at the scene of a shooting or not: all gun crime was perceived to be AK crime. The Columbine shootings may be regarded as the notorious peak of the assaults committed by embittered social misfits in the era of the Kalashnikov culture, but there were many other appalling instances of the phenomenon.

Two years earlier, for instance, on 17 January 1989, Patrick Purdy had taken a Chinese 56 AK—a gun he had been able to buy legally over the counter in Oregon—to the Cleveland Elementary School in Stockton, California. Unusually, the rifle was equipped with a two-drum, biscuit-tin-shaped magazine which held two lots of seventy-five rounds. The drum magazine had been developed by Norinco technicians in China to increase the individual firepower of People's Army infantrymen. This was very specifically a battlefield weapon, although it had proved unpopular with many People's Army and Vietnamese communist troops who found it bulky and heavy, which limited its manoeuvrability. It did, however, enable the soldier to deliver a fearsome wall of fire in combat. Clearly a weapon of this kind was totally out of place in suburban America, yet Purdy was able to buy the drums as well as his rifle over the same gunshop counter. He strode into the school grounds and emptied both drums. When he was finished five children were dead, twenty-nine were injured and one teacher was wounded; carnage enough for Purdy's efforts to be dubbed the Stockton schoolyard massacre. In September the same year Joseph Wesbecker, the disgruntled ex-employee of urban myth and in this case terrible actuality, took an AK47 into an office in Louisville, Kentucky, killing seven and wounding thirteen before he turned the gun on himself.

After the Caltrans Maintenance Yard fired Arturo Reyes Torres for theft in December 1997 he responded by taking an AK47 to work. He killed four and wounded two. In 2000 Michael McDermott, aggrieved that back taxes were going to be taken out of wages, fired forty-nine rounds from his AK47 at colleagues at Edgewater Technology in Massachusetts. He killed seven before he ran out of ammunition, which happens swiftly when firing a Kalashnikov on full automatic. When fire finally ended the fifty-one-day siege of the Branch Davidian complex in Waco, Texas on 19 April 1993, officers from the Bureau of Alcohol, Tobacco and Firearms and the FBI found forty-four AK47s inside the smoking ruins where the cult's leader, David Koresh, had made his last stand.

But it was an attack twelve weeks before the slaughter at Waco that finally forced the US government into action, and it incorporated elements that would, within ten years, bring the AK to worldwide attention. Mir

Aimal Kasi, a Pakistani Muslim resident in the USA who had grown increasingly outraged by the treatment of the Palestinians by Israel and by what he perceived as America's unflinching support for Israel, chose to express his outrage violently. He struck at the heart of the American security establishment: CIA headquarters in Langley, Virginia.

Kasi was not a member of any terrorist group. When he launched his attack it was as a lone assailant, although those unfortunate enough to be outside the CIA buildings on 25 January 1993 would learn that no one with an AK is truly alone. A lone gunman with an AK—especially one attacking unarmed civilians—has an attacking force out of proportion to his individual status. When Kasi pulled up in a flat-back pick-up truck at a set of traffic lights by the CIA headquarters during the morning rush hour he had become, in effect, his own terrorist organization.

With what appeared to be preternatural coolness for a man who was holding an automatic weapon, Kasi stepped out of his truck, briefly looked around the stationary cars that surrounded it, brought his AK up to his chest and calmly began to shoot into the vehicles. There were none of the shouts or screams that are often heard from men in combat. Those who watched him were amazed by his calmness—Kasi simply stood by his truck and fired haphazardly at the surrounding vehicles and their occupants. He showed no emotion; perhaps he was hypnotized by the power of his gun.

Kasi fired for no more than a minute, hitting five cars with eleven bullets. Then, just as calmly as he had got out, he got back into his truck and pulled away. Behind him a normal traffic jam had been transformed into a smoking, screaming glimpse of America's far-off wars. Kasi's short spree wounded three victims and killed two CIA employees, Lansing Bennett, sixty-six, and Frank Darling, twenty-eight. Miraculously Darling's wife, who was sitting alongside him, survived.

The attack on the CIA headquarters was an attack too far for the government. The USA could live with a high homicide rate, but it could not ignore such a murderous assault on one of the central pillars of the state's authority. In September 1994 President Bill Clinton signed into law the Federal Assault Weapons Ban, making it illegal to sell or buy 'semi-automatic assault weapons' for a ten-year period. Section 921 (a) (30), Title 18 (USC) of the bill was very specific about AK-type weapons, naming as illegal 'any of the firearms, or copies or duplicates of the firearms in any caliber, known as; Norinco, Mitchell, Poly Technologies, Avtomat Kalashnikovs'.

The intentions may have been good, but the legislation itself was not well thought out. Due to the wording of some parts of the bill America's gun merchants were still able to trade in AKs. The bill referred only to weapons manufactured after the date of the ban; weapons made wholly, or produced in kit form, before 1994 could still be legally sold. This was not the only hole in the bill's provisions. One of the specific definitions of an assault rifle was that it should be a weapon with a pistol-grip handle. Manufacturers responded by using wooden thumbhole stocks that swept forward to join the pistol grip and create one smooth form with a hole for the trigger. Technically this made even a brand-new AK legal, and such guns were promoted by gun clubs and rifle associations as 'sporting weapons'. The magazines could fit both pre-ban AKs and adapted post-ban 'sporting' versions—though why a sportsman would need to fire seventy-five rounds at a time was seldom asked. The bill also proscibed any magazine that held more than ten rounds, but because the same time limitations applied to magazines as to the rifles themselves, the kind of drums used to such deadly effect by Patrick Purdy at the Stockton schoolyard shootings were still legal, as they had been manufactured before the ban. It also meant that magazines manufactured before 1994 were imported from the former Eastern Bloc. Desperate for foreign currency, governments in newly capitalist eastern Europe exported the only thing they had that the Americans wanted: cheap guns. Thousands of AKs and mountains of ammunition made their way on to the market as Bulgaria, Hungary and Yugoslavia found a ready market for their stockpiles.

If the bill was meant to take AKs off the streets of America, it was destined to be a failure from its inception. It could even be argued that it put more AKs into general circulation, and as they circulated they sank down through the strata of American society to find a natural home where society was breaking down. It would be in the chaos of black America's streets where the Kalashnikov would do its dirtiest work, and its presence was soon reflected in a black youth culture predominantly built around the confrontational and aggressive sounds of hip-hop and rap.

The AK would prove itself just as attractive to the arbiters of rap culture at the turn of the millennium as it had been to the left-wing intelligentsia in the late 1960s and the Soviet propaganda industry in the late 1940s. In the AK rap had found an instant shorthand for some of its central concerns—respect, firepower and rebellion. Hip-hop often claims to be an artistic representation of the reality of the streets it came from, but to the innocent ear it could sound like a sexist and murderous call to arms. In Cypress Hill's gangsta rap *cri de coeur* 'A To The K' the group made it clear that the AK47 was an essential part of the urban armoury: 'You heard it on the radio, you seen it on the TV show. A to the K? A to the motherfuckin' Z.' Even sex could be catered for by the quasi-phallic bend of the magazine, and in 'Heated Heavy' rap artist Krayzie Bone made the obvious psychological connection between the power of the gun and the power of the penis: 'Runnin' with the AK-47 bucking, heated heavy/ nigga love the way I wet 'em when I get up in 'em.' To 'wet' someone is to spill their blood; to 'get up in' someone is to fuck them.

Once the AK had insinuated its way into popular culture it became self-replicating. Its revolutionary credentials allowed performers to portray it as a weapon of the macho self-reliant black man and a brand of resistance. It was simultaneously the gun of the street and an essentially anti-establishment weapon—a weapon that had already taken on the might of the US government in Vietnam and won, and was now resisting that superpower in the Middle East and Africa. The instant respect and status that the AK offered to young men who otherwise received little or no recognition from society at large or even their immediate peers was expressed succinctly by Ice Cube on N.W.A.'s *Straight Outta Compton*, an album that presented America with an anguished and angry shout from black America's violent and desperate streets. 'AK47 is the tool,' he warned.

'Don't make me act the motherfuckin' fool.'

The tragically low level of provocation that was required for a young black male to use his AK47 was made clear by Eazy-E, who proclaimed what he would do to anyone who attempted to steal his car: 'Cuz I pack the tech 9 plus an AK-47/ Send a one-way ticket to my hell or maybe heaven.' In this prickly mix of crime and braggadocio no slight could go unnoticed, no offence unpunished. It was a world in which respect was everything, and few things demand more respect than a loaded AK47. Hold it in your hand and the world lowers its eyes. It was from this culture of AK worship and a murderously wayward understanding of when it is appropriate to open fire with an automatic weapon that Steven Williams, an eighteen-year-old member of a New Orleans gang, emerged.

By 2003 gun crime in New Orleans had become so prevalent and wild that the city had gained the unofficial title of 'the nation's murder capital'. Like other American cities it had long suffered from gun crime, but the introduction of crack cocaine to a society armed with Kalashnikovs established a whole new and flamboyant way of killing people. Something snapped in the consciousness of the gunmen and, not content with being merely criminals, they turned into esoteric and exhibitionist figures that belonged as much to comic books as they did to the streets, driving at each other with AKs blazing from their car windows in a modern version of the medieval joust. The shooting became maddened and indiscriminate—women, children and old people were caught in the street as cars full of young male gang-bangers unloaded AKs at each other and the city descended into a chaos and supercharged misery that was extreme even in the violent culture of urban America.

There were thirty murders in New Orleans in April 2003, the deadliest month in a year which would see 275 homicide victims in the city. The killing was not city-wide but concentrated in just seven of the nearly 500 square kilometres that came under the jurisdiction of the New Orleans authorities. That small area consisted of the poor black neighbourhoods and social housing projects where unemployment was high and drug abuse rife. Black teenagers had two immediate goals—making money and staying alive. The two came together in drugs, and dealing drugs naturally led to gangs.

The city was divided into a number of wards, each with one preponderant gang that held the turf and ran the crime. These main gangs had cadet branches whose members—kids as young as thirteen—aped the behaviour of their elders and hoped, by being noted for their aggression or acquisitiveness, to rise through the ranks. At fifteen you were old enough to be a street soldier in New Orleans; at twenty-five you were a veteran. When officers of the New Orleans Police Department (NOPD) came into the housing projects to look for drugs, weapons or suspects they came heavily armed, carrying handguns and shotguns that could knock a man flat. It was a powerful configuration but one that still left the officers at a disadvantage if they came up against a man, or boy, armed with an assault rifle. Consequently the police did not come into the worst wards unless they had to and New Orleans' most troubled ghettoes were left outside the law, their reputation for violence and drugs becoming a self-fulfilling prophecy.

Often high on crack, gunmen from these areas whom the police did encounter would often offer themselves as targets, coming out of buildings with their AKs blazing or, in that seemingly irresistible action of the AK owner, showing the weapon's profile to the enemy. Since a gunman on crack is not to be reasoned with, the police would sit back and call in special sniper units to shoot him. Most units had no compunction about doing this, but it further increased the atmosphere of siege and violence in the wards and turned young people especially against the police.

The city authorities were attempting to clear this fearsome list of social problems with the wrecking ball, knocking down hundred-year-old tenements and decaying 1970s public housing projects alike. But the authorities were tainted with corruption in the eyes of many of the citizens, and in the black wards people were convinced they were being moved out so that white property developers could move in. So as well as drugs and gang tensions there was seething resentment towards City Hall in the wards. The police were regularly fired on, and as April approached the murder rate threatened to go off the scale. Yet this was an internalized anger—the majority of fatal shootings were black on black. As early as 1992 the rap group Bone Thugs-N-Harmony could sing, 'Hell yeah! It's that same nigga runnin' with the AK-47. Bustin niggas in the belly.' The belly was a bad place to be busted by an AK47.

Small disputes were rendered big by the simmering rage in the city. New Orleans' gang members were willing to employ levels of violence reminiscent of the West Bank or the Sudan. Yet the city authorities seemed willing to let it happen as long as the gunfire was confined to poor black areas. But it is very hard to confine automatic weapon fire and even districts such as Central City would resound with the pop-pop-pop of automatic gunfire. By April 2003 it had become so bad that the NOPD was forced to call upon the help of the US Marshals' Service and the FBI. The marshals were brought in to track down suspects, and the FBI to prepare federal cases against the worst of the gunmen. This, theoretically, would leave the NOPD free to concentrate on keeping a lid on the young hotheads who were firing AKs in the streets of a major American city.

Afro-American Steven Williams was just such a hothead from the wards. He had been running with a gang for five years, since he was thirteen, but had recently stepped up to take over the leadership. Opportunities for promotion came regularly in a city with New Orleans' murder rate, but Williams' authority was reinforced by his Bulgarian AK and, as far as his fellow gang members understood it, his absolute willingness to use that weapon.

A week before Williams' AK would gain him notoriety and a life prison sentence, another member of the gang, eighteen-year-old Hilliard 'Head' Smith, had been gunned down in the street and killed. Williams and his fellow gang members did not know who the murderer was, but they did know who had pulled the trigger the year before when Smith had been shot and wounded. They knew because twelve months later fifteen-year-old Jonathan 'Caveman' Williams (no relation) was still boasting that he had been the gunman. Caveman, as his nickname suggested, was a big youth, but teenagers are prone to exaggeration and Caveman had never been charged with the shooting. Whether it was true or not, it was enough to condemn him to death.

At just past 10.30 a.m. on Monday, 14 April, Williams and four other gang members—Tyrone Crump and Michelle Fulton, both seventeen, Herbert Everett, eighteen, and Ralph Enclade, nineteen, arrived in two cars at the John McDonogh High School Gymnasium. The gang members were dressed identically in jeans and white t-shirts, and all five wore their hair in dreadlocks. One of the boys carried a pistol, Williams his AK.

Known to its thousand or so students as John Mac, the school stands two kilometres north of the French Quarter, on a tree-lined street alongside Esplanade Avenue, the four-lane highway that leads from the docks to the north-western edge of the city. As the projects had been pulled down and redeveloped, the children of the rehoused population were sent to John Mac and took their ward loyalties with them. Warring gangs that had formerly been a kilometre apart now found themselves going to the same school. Invariably this led to conflict, which in turn led to confusion as the violence and drug-selling within the school attracted the attention of older adolescents and John Mac spiralled out of its teachers' control. On the day that Williams and his gang arrived at the school, out of the twelve hundred kids on the premises there were at least three hundred that the teachers could not positively identify as their own students. John Mac had become a chaotic arena for gang violence and intimidation, an institution in a vacuum—as had numerous other schools.

The city had attempted to address the problem. Its education department had an annual security budget of $4 million to spend on twenty senior schools. John Mac had been equipped with security fences and had four guards to cover the two entrances and operate the metal detectors that were supposed to stop pupils bringing weapons in. There was also a full-time New Orleans police officer on the premises. But in the chaos of John Mac, policing, like teaching, had become a matter of holding the line. The guards stuck to their positions, scanning bags and patting down students; they did not walk around the security fence that morning. If they had patrolled the school's perimeter, they would have discovered a hole in the fence. After pulling up in their cars Williams and his gang simply stepped through the hole and on to the school grounds.

Different people have different memories of that morning in the John Mac gymnasium. Some recalled Caveman joking and holding court, while others didn't notice him at all; but several witnesses agree that at some point a girl persuaded him to sit in a chair next to the gymnasium entrance. Again, memories are confused as to exactly which girl persuaded Caveman to move. Perhaps he was so concerned with acting the part of a big guy, a gangsta, in front of his peers that he failed to be suspicious when he needed to be. Perhaps he was attracted to the girl who betrayed him. Either way, Caveman sat by the door.

Williams and his gang were not students at John Mac, but they had gang members or associates who were, and as well as persuading Caveman to move, one of these insiders guided the assailants by mobile phone to the door of the gymnasium. In the general confusion of John Mac no one stopped the identically dressed gang from entering the building or questioned their right to be on the premises. Neither did anyone see the AK47 that Williams carried flat against his side and under his jacket.

There were two hundred students inside the gymnasium when Williams strode through the doors. Immediately he brought the AK up to waist height and aimed it at Caveman. It took several seconds of shouting and confusion before the distinct outline of his AK was recognized throughout the room and the dismayed cries of 'He's got a gun!' went up. No one inside the gymnasium needed a lesson in the effects of a Kalashnikov—they had seen the damage AKs caused even in open spaces, and knew only too well that in a confined space the hail of fire it released would be undiscriminating and deadly.

Caveman froze in his seat as the gang gathered in front of him. Face to face with his doom the fifteen-year-old began to plead for his life, but Williams' reaction was contemptuous: he laughed at the boy's pleas and cursed him. The rest of the gang joined in, mocking Caveman's terror. Then Williams emptied half a magazine into his victim's body. But even though the barrel of the AK was within a few metres of Caveman, not all

Williams' shots hit the target. This could have been due to the sheer excitement, the rage of the moment, nerves or carelessness. But more probably Williams was holding his AK in a self-consciously gangsta style— shooting with one hand rather than two—to add an aesthetic of gang bravado to the assault that would make his triumph over Caveman complete and render the shooting truly memorable for the onlookers. The first burst of fire put eight bullets into Caveman's torso and wounded three girls: one fifteen-year-old was shot in both legs, a sixteen-year-old was hit in the thigh and another sixteen-year-old was shot on her buttocks and left arm. A fourth, pregnant, girl was crushed when the students rushed to get out of Williams' line of fire. As the space around Caveman cleared Williams stood over him and at point blank range fired another burst directly into the fifteen-year-old's head. The first burst had hit most of his vital organs and knocked him to the floor: he was already fatally wounded, if not dead. The second burst from Williams' AK removed his face, guaranteeing that Caveman's family would not be able to display his body in an open coffin.

The whole episode was a callous and highly dramatized act, a murder that perfectly represented the horrific bravado of gang warfare and the transformative power of the AK47. Williams had entered the room as a nineteen-year-old hood with a grudge and an AK47. He left it as a killer, a man worthy of fear and respect. In destroying Caveman's face he had saved his own.

The attackers fled the school by the hole in the fence, but were apprehended near by. Within minutes anguished parents had gathered at the school gates, desperate for a sight of their children and angrily asking where the guards had been when the killers had entered the school. But this was no Columbine, no lunatic rampage by the existentially challenged children of the middle classes, a dark fantasy made real in the heart of an essentially privileged community. This was ordinary life in New Orleans, a city that had joined Ramallah and Baghdad on the international roster of AK municipalities.

The Rev. Thompson Norwood Jr, fresh from organizing a public gun buy-back, an arrangement by which young men were encouraged to hand in weapons for dollars, arrived at the school in despair. 'I'm amazed that this type of weapon is on the street,' he said. 'I don't know where our young people get that type of weapon. You think of those over in Afghanistan or Iraq.' But the rest of the USA soon forgot any shock it had felt on learning that owning an AK was easy for a nineteen-year-old boy. New Orleans and its black residents—a population that had been living through a virtual civil war amongst its young men—were left with further evidence that America wasn't really interested in what black youths did to black youths as long as they kept it to themselves. However, the killing of Caveman had a galvanizing effect on the city itself. The NOPD, obliged to admit that it had lost control of whole sections of the city, stepped up its seizures of illegal weapons. The police took possession of hundreds of handguns, rifles and shotguns. But few AKs.

A month after Williams executed Caveman, Gladys Dyson, an eighteen-year-old black girl who had finished her school exams the week before, was walking along Washington Avenue when two cars drove up the street at high speed. Gunmen inside both vehicles opened fire with AKs. Panicking, Dyson started to run, but the cars continued to come in her direction, the occupants firing wildly at each other. As they raced past, an AK round hit her. People had become so inured to life on New Orleans' streets under the rule of crack and AKs that a year later, at the trial of the three young black men charged with Dyson's manslaughter, her older sister didn't bemoan the lawlessness so much as her sister's reaction to gunfire. If Gladys had lain down rather than running when she first heard shots, said her sister, she would still be alive. 'When I hear shooting now,' she added, 'I just get down on the ground.'

It was understandable if Rev. Thompson Norwood Jr considered Kalashnikov gun battles to be the preserve of desolate Third World war zones, but New Orleans was about to become as desolate as a Third World war zone itself. In the week that followed the devastating arrival of Hurricane Katrina and the disastrous failure of the 17th Street canal levee on 28 August 2005, the city's social order rapidly broke down. As downtown New Orleans filled with water and the poor black population was effectively left to its own devices, looters began to wade through the floods and many of them were carrying AKs. The gun's under-engineered workings were impervious to the damp that was insinuating itself into every bit of machinery in the city, from microwaves to power plants. New Orleans under water was, like Vietnam and Iraq, a situation for which the Kalashnikov could have been designed: it was an opportunity for the AK to make a step change and move forward again. A police officer described the atmosphere in New Orleans as one of 'nervous energy'—an atmosphere, in fact, that usually accompanies the AK, to be replaced by terror when the rifle does its worst work.

When the rule of law broke down across the city, the AK was waiting in the wings. Even the smallest tear in the social fabric is enough for it to gain entry, so a flood is an open door to a weapon that flourishes amidst disaster. An abandoned populace helped itself to food and in some cases guns, but there was not, as some newspapers claimed at the time, a glut of looted AKs in New Orleans. The downtown Wal-Mart on Tchoupitoulas Street was looted, but although Wal-Mart sells arms, it does not sell AKs or AK derivatives. The looters were stealing wide-screen TVs, computers, bicycles (of dubious use in a flooded city) and jewellery rather than firearms. There were several other gun shops in the flooded area but there were very few AKs in cases waiting to be stolen by looters. In truth, the population of New Orleans was armed with AKs before Katrina stuck.

Looters rushed to take advantage of the vacuum left by the NOPD officers who were engaged in rescue work, and Louisiana police officers brought in to plug this hole in the city's law enforcement operation were fired on by gunmen with AKs. One team of gunmen, operating in a pair as in the Middle East, came out of the French Quarter just before midnight and fired directly into the window of a police station. These skirmishes with the AK-carrying locals persuaded Mayor Ray Nagin to put fifteen hundred police officers back on the street in a direct law enforcement role. Initially the officers of the NOPD, often leaderless and unsure whether they would be backed up if they got in trouble, had opted to avoid gun battles with looters: there were reports that some of the looters were themselves police officers, and they knew also that without specialist firearms units they would be out-gunned if they encountered an AK. Television cameras pointed down on the flooded city from their helicopters and picked out lone individuals. Angry, black and in open revolt, men with similar fire in their eyes to Palestinian militiamen or Iraqi insurgents waved their AKs in defiance. The gunmen were no less criminal than they had been before they were caught on film, but the gun had a transformative effect. New Orleans' gang-bangers were becoming Third World revolutionaries.

In Vietnam, the sight of black-clad NVA troops carrying the gun into battle had signified the war against imperialism—the young, utterly committed fighter armed only with a pair of sandals to walk in and an AK to kill Americans. Now the banana-shaped magazine could have been designed with the lightweight digital camera in mind. As the television news crew choppers swept over the flooded streets and the AK made one of its characteristic shifts of image on the TV screens of America, the weapon of the gang-banger and the drug dealer, the weapon that had cut mercilessly through John Mac two years previously, morphed into a sign of resistance to white America's indifference, local corruption and government racism. Before the flood the AK had been the curse of New Orleans, after the flood some citizens saw it as their saviour. In the absence of effective law and order, people took advantage of the opportunity to settle scores. In a bleak re-enactment of Cypress Hill's 'A To The K', a well-known drug dealer had his limousine flagged down as he attempted to get out of the flooded centre of the city and head for high ground. The door was opened and the interior sprayed with AK fire. The AK and two spent magazine cases bound together with tape for quick reload were found at the scene. The second magazine was unnecessary, because at such close range the drug dealer's body would have been effectively shredded by the bullets in the first burst; perhaps it was done for effect.

The AK continued to take advantage of the city's weakened state. Almost a year after Hurricane Katrina, in May 2006, a schizophrenic male who had failed to take his medication and whose family had desperately but unsuccessfully sought psychological and medical help in a city that could barely help itself, picked up an AK and started shooting in the Algiers district. The police stood off for six hours, then killed him. A spokesman for the New Orleans Forensic Center commented, 'When the police department is forced to do the job that the mental health system should do, it's a lose-lose for everybody.'

Slowly New Orleans recovered, and federal money and a reinvigorated NOPD restored some law and order to the previously flooded streets, forcing the gunmen back into the projects and wards from which they had emerged. But it doesn't take a flood to allow the AK to take over a city centre, and a country need not be as destabilized as Sudan, Palestine or Chechnya. It is enough to allow sections of a city to fall into desperate poverty and by marketing the Kalashnikov America opened the door to a gun that excels wherever social cohesion is compromised.

America loves brands and it had turned the AK47 into the Coca-Cola of small arms, a brand that infiltrated the consciousness of the planet. In a paradigm that any marketing executive would hope to achieve the Kalashnikov reached critical mass in the world market for assault rifles, becoming a self-replicating presence on the TV news and in combat zones that spilled across the boundaries of conflict and current affairs. The process was even reflected back to Russia where, in 2004, entrepreneur and ex-rock star Andrey Koltakov launched an MP3 player with an exterior modelled on an AK ammunition magazine that, when attached to an AK47, pumps music into a headset rather than bullets into a body. Koltakov declared, 'This is our bit for world peace. Hopefully, from now on many militants and terrorists will use their AK-47s to listen to music and audio books. They need to chill out.' Perhaps, but if the militants did chill out the AK would lose its greatest advertising platform. Conflicts are the heritage on which the Kalashnikov brand is built.

Previously, globalization had been about the imposition of American products on a worldwide market. The Kalashnikov has changed that. It is the world's first truly global product, operating on its own terms, floating above the mix of cultures and countries that could make a claim for it, be that Russia responsibility for its genesis or the sheer gusto and scale that China had brought to its mass production. Because its points of origin are now so disparate—workshops in Pakistan and factories in Cuba, to name but two—the AK47 is a truly international phenomenon. Above old notions of belonging it floats on a tide of death and money: narcotics money, CIA money, Saudi money and Russian money. Keeping tabs on the driving forces behind the millions of AKs in the world is like trying to catch a bullet—it can't be done.

At the beginning of *First Blood II* an American comments on the armoury that Rambo has chosen for his mission: 'A beat-to-shit AK? Every twelve-year-old in Nam's got one of those.' To which Rambo's reply is: 'Exactly'.

By 2004 America's inner cities were heading in the same direction. In the end even the USA is not safe from the Kalashnikov. It makes the rules now.

ACKNOWLEDGEMENTS

With great thanks to Patricia McDonald Hodges, Emmy Hodges, Damian and Alice Bird, Bill Borrows, Clare Conville, Teddy Crane and Chloe McCulloch, Grant Fleming, John Florey, Jocasta Hamilton, Emmanuel Jal, Mikhail Kalashnikov and family, Peter Moszynski, Gordon Thomson and, especially, Anna Crane.

NORTH COUNTRY LIBRARY SYSTEM
Watertown, New York

CENTRAL LIBRARY
WATERTOWN

OCT   2008

BAKER & TAYLOR